DON'T
MISS THIS

IN THE
BOOK OF MORMON

DON'T MISS THIS

IN THE
BOOK OF MORMON

EXPLORING ONE VERSE FROM EACH CHAPTER

EMILY BELLE FREEMAN
and DAVID BUTLER

DESERET
BOOK

Salt Lake City, Utah

Library of Congress Cataloging-in-Publication Data

Names: Freeman, Emily, 1969– author. | Butler, David (Seminary teacher), author.
Title: Don't miss this in The Book of Mormon : exploring one verse from each chapter / Emily Belle Freeman and David Butler.
Description: Salt Lake City, Utah : Deseret Book, [2019] | Includes bibliographical references. | Summary: "A collection of 239 short devotional-style lessons exploring one verse from each chapter of the Book of Mormon"—Provided by publisher.
Identifiers: LCCN 2019038733 | ISBN 9781629727042 (trade paperback)
Subjects: LCSH: Book of Mormon—Commentaries. | LCGFT: Meditations.
Classification: LCC BX8627 .F74 2019 | DDC 289.3/22—dc23
LC record available at https://lccn.loc.gov/2019038733

Printed in the United States of America
Brigham Young University Press, Provo, UT

10   9   8   7   6   5   4   3   2

To my mother, Leslie Oswald, who loves
the Book of Mormon more than anyone I know,
and who passed that love down to me.
—EBF

To my Jenny, who has His image
in her countenance.
—DB

INTRODUCTION

Greg, Megan, and I (Emily) once spent a day at Disneyland in the company of a tour guide who wore a checkered vest. The man was an expert at knowing which rides to go on early in the day, where we should stop for lunch, and where to get the best treats in the park. But one of my favorite things about the guide was that he would stop us periodically to show us things most people might not ever notice. For example, have you ever discovered the tiny little house built next to the roots of the very big tree that stands just outside the line for the Indiana Jones ride? "Oh!" our guide would exclaim as we walked through certain parts of the park. "You don't want to miss this!" We would stop, and look, and learn. We loved that day! It was one of our favorite journeys we have ever taken through Disneyland.

For the purpose of this book, maybe you can imagine we are taking a similar tour through the Book of Mormon. If you want to imagine David in a checkered vest, that's even more fun. We may not be the greatest experts on the context and content of every single chapter, but there are definitely things we don't want you to miss! So we have chosen one powerful verse from every chapter in the Book of Mormon, one of our favorites, and we hope it will become one of yours. Sometimes we've even just chosen a phrase from a scripture that had special meaning for us; at other times, we've included a passage that carries on for more than one verse. If you wonder whose choices are whose, just check for our initials at the bottom of each chapter.

It is our hope that as you study, you won't just focus on our favorite verses but will also find some of your own: powerful verses that you can hold on to for answers, direction, and comfort. This is so important to us that we have actually included a spot at the bottom of every single page for you to write down your own favorite scripture from that chapter. We hope as you read there will be moments when you will say, "Oh! I'm so glad I didn't miss this!" Perhaps, by the end, this will become one of your favorite journeys through the Book of Mormon.

The devotionals in this book are meant to be read alongside your Book of Mormon. We hope the lessons, stories, and daily reflection questions will help supplement your experience and open your eyes to things you may never have noticed before. That is our prayer for you. We are so excited to embark on this journey together. In addition to this book, we will be sharing weekly messages on YouTube, and you can find more things you don't want to miss at www.dontmissthisstudy.com.

We wish this book could have come with a pineapple Dole Whip and ended with a firework show, but instead we send our love, our encouragement, and our hope that this study of the Book of Mormon will be one of your fondest yet.

Enjoy this journey!

David and Emily

1 NEPHI 1:20

But behold, I, Nephi, **will show unto you that the tender mercies of the Lord** are over all those whom he hath chosen, because of their faith, to make them mighty even unto the power of deliverance.

The Book of Mormon begins with an invitation tucked away at the end of the first chapter. Nephi explains that he wants to show us that the tender mercies of the Lord are over all those whom He has chosen. Tender mercies that come from faith, that make us mighty, that deliver us.

One year when I was teaching seminary, I invited the kids in my class to look for a tender mercy in every chapter of the Book of Mormon. We spent the year looking for the experiences in which the people were made mighty and delivered from a hard situation. Every morning, one student would get up and share a tender mercy he or she had discovered in the reading the night before. It was an awesome experience . . . one you might want to try for this whole year with your family. One of my favorites came as a surprise. It was at the very beginning of the year. A ninth-grade girl stood up at the front of the class and said, "It was a tender mercy that Laman and Lemuel left Jerusalem and went into the wilderness with their family." I had never thought of that before. But she was right—for Lehi and Sariah, the fact that Laman and Lemuel actually left Jerusalem behind was a tender mercy. That year was filled to the brim with tender-mercy moments.

At the end of the Book of Mormon, Moroni closes with an invitation very similar to the one that Nephi began the Book of Mormon with: "Behold, I would exhort you that when ye shall read these things . . . that ye would remember how merciful the Lord hath been unto the children of men . . ." (Moroni 10:3). Remember His mercies. —EBF

Reflect and Respond

As you read the Book of Mormon this year, watch for the tender mercies of the Lord in every chapter.

Your favorite scripture in 1 Nephi 1

1 NEPHI 2:16

Wherefore, **I did cry unto the Lord**;
and behold he did visit me.

My friend lived and worked on a dairy farm growing up, which meant he was assigned several jobs and chores that he dreaded. One of those was moving pipes in the middle of the night to be sure the land and cattle got the water they needed. One early morning, about 2:00 a.m., he went out to move the pipes and got the truck stuck in a ditch. He tried and tried to get it out, but no luck! He sat in the bed of the truck, tired, cold, and covered in mud, and wondered to himself: *Who can I call for help?* No one was awake. He was out in the mud. There aren't many people willing or able at a time and situation like that. But, instinctively, he thought of his dad. He called him on the cell phone and woke him up. The conversation was simple. "Dad, I need help." The answer was a groggy but willing, "I'll be right there." Within ten minutes, my friend's dad had come with a tractor and a tow line to get him out.

Not many people have permission to wake up a hardworking farmer in the middle of the night and expect or even get a response. But a son can. Children always have permission. And they can always expect an answer.

Nephi knew this too. He had a need—a desire. He felt like he was stuck and out in the cold in his search for truth. So he cried unto His Father for help, and, just like you would expect a father would—the Lord came and visited His son.

God is always available. He is willing and able and anxious to hear our pleas and come to our relief. It's what fathers do. —DB

Reflect and Respond

When you cry unto the Father for help, what are some of the different ways He might answer you?

Your favorite scripture in 1 Nephi 2

1 NEPHI 3:5

And now, behold thy brothers murmur, saying **it is a hard thing** which I have required of them; but behold I have not required it of them, but it is a commandment of the Lord.

What is the hardest thing you have ever done? Perhaps your life has been filled with so many hard things it is difficult to choose. The scriptures teach us over and over again that hard things can make us stronger. They can prepare us for other things God has in store.

Many years ago, our family decided to try walking from the Draper Utah Temple to the Salt Lake Temple. It was a twenty-six-mile walk. We prepared for months beforehand. It took us eight hours, including a stop for lunch, but we all made it. When we arrived at the temple, we felt we had accomplished something remarkable.

Several years later, our son Josh was serving a mission in Atlanta, Georgia. One Monday in the middle of the month he wrote home and told us that because of some unexpected events, they were out of miles on their car, and they would have to walk to all of their appointments for the remainder of the month. One of those appointments was quite far from their apartment. It would be a fifteen-mile walk round trip. "But don't worry," he told us, "I know I can walk that far. Once my mom made us walk twenty-six miles in one day."

I'll be honest, I teared up when I read those words. He knew he could do hard things because we had accomplished something harder. That hard thing had prepared him for what was ahead. —EBF

Reflect and Respond

Do something hard this week. Take on a challenge. Stretch yourself. Write about your experience.

Your favorite scripture in 1 Nephi 3

1 NEPHI 4:7

Nevertheless I went forth . . .

This is the moment when Nephi tells us he went forth needing to be led by the Spirit because he didn't know what to do. I have experienced moments like that. Have you?

It was late one afternoon when the call came. A dear friend was returning home from the hospital with a baby boy who was very, very ill. The doctors had honored the family's wish to let the baby pass away at home. I was saddened by the news. Heartbroken. The Spirit whispered, *You should go there.*

Not right now, I responded back. I can't go now. They have just returned home. They need time to settle in.

You should go. Again, the message was clear.

I'll take dinner over tonight, I answered. When things calm down. It will be better.

You should go now. The Spirit was unmistakable.

So I turned my car around and began driving to their home. I felt like the timing was wrong; I felt uncomfortable about showing up. *Nevertheless I went forth.*

I won't ever forget knocking on the door that afternoon, and how the baby's mother and grandmother opened the door and expressed so much gratitude that I was there. They were about to have a family prayer to end their fast. The whole family wanted to gather together in the family room, but someone needed to sit in the baby's room and hold him because he was hooked up to all the medical machines. So I sat in the room, and I held that sweet baby for twenty minutes while the family gathered together to petition the Lord for strength to face what was ahead. I consider that moment as one of the sweetest moments of my life, and what if I hadn't gone? —EBF

....

Reflect and Respond

Make a conscious effort to respond to the Spirit this week, even when it doesn't make sense. Nevertheless, go forth.

Your favorite scripture in 1 Nephi 4

_____

_____

1 NEPHI 5:8

And she spake, saying: Now **I know of a surety** that the Lord hath
commanded my husband to flee into the wilderness; yea, and I also know
of a surety that the Lord hath protected my sons, and delivered them.

Sariah, the wife of the prophet Lehi, left her home, her friends, her routines, her favorite shops—everything—and went out into the wilderness with nothing but tents and trust that her husband was being directed by the Lord. Then she let her sons go on a wildly dangerous mission with that same kind of trust. Sometime later, that trust and faith became a surety.

We once left on a long family vacation and had not gotten very far when the questions started coming from the passenger's seat: "Did you shut off the lights in the bathroom?" "Yes." "Are you sure?" "Positive." "Did you bring the garbage cans out front?" "Yes." "Are you sure?" "Positive." "Did you lock the front door?" "Pretty sure." "Pretty sure?" "Yeah, I am pretty sure." That didn't cut it. We turned around. I walked up and checked the door, which was locked. Then I was sure—and we all went on the rest of the trip with a lot more peace.

Trusting in a forgetful spouse can be difficult—especially considering I have such a bad track record for remembering to lock the front door. Trusting the Lord is easier—especially because of His track record. He is a God of consistent miracles. But, as with Sariah, through time, that trust can become a surety. The Lord can let us grow and become refined in our believing for a time, and then He can give us a witness that moves us to surety. That surety will bring added peace and confidence. —DB

Reflect and Respond

What are the things you "know of a surety"? How do you know?

Your favorite
scripture in
1 Nephi 5

1 NEPHI 6:4

For the fulness of mine intent is that I may persuade
men to come unto **the God of Abraham, and the God
of Isaac, and the God of Jacob**, and be saved.

Ours is a personal God, one who responds to individual needs in singular ways.
Consider the role of God in the lives of Abraham, Isaac, and Jacob.

The story of Abraham is filled with promises—the promise of a son, the promise of
priesthood, the promise of a land of his own. Among other things, Abraham's God was
a God of Promises.

Abraham's son was Isaac. The most unforgettable moment of the story of Isaac comes
after a long hike up Mount Moriah, after an altar was built, and after a sacrifice had been
prepared. Then there was a ram in the thicket and a miracle in just the right moment. In
that moment, for Isaac, God was a God of Deliverance.

Isaac had a son named Jacob. Unlike his father and grandfather, Jacob's life was filled
with deceiving. Through each experience, Jacob struggled between trying to solve the
problem on his own and learning how to wait on the Lord and trust His promises.
Eventually God changed Jacob's name to Israel—after he had struggled with God and
man and finally overcome (see Genesis 32:28). For Jacob, God came as a God of Second
Chances.

Whenever I come across the words "the God of Abraham, the God of Isaac, the God
of Jacob," I change them to read instead, "a God of Promises, a God of Deliverance, a
God of Second Chances." A God who responds to individual needs in singular and personal ways. —EBF

Reflect and Respond

*How has God responded to the specific needs of your life through
individual experiences?*

Your favorite
scripture in
1 Nephi 6

1 NEPHI 7:10-11

How is it that ye have forgotten that ye have seen an angel
of the Lord? Yea, and how is it that ye have forgotten what great
things the Lord hath done for us, in delivering us . . . ?

One night my wife and I opened up our missionary journals and let the kids take turns choosing a random date, and then we read them what we wrote for that day. (There was a rule established at the beginning of the game that we could veto a day or a line just in case we had not been in the best of moods when we wrote a particular entry or if it was too personal to share—usually the first!)

Someone chose a day, and I flipped to the page and started reading. Oh, the memories came flooding back! I could smell the food carts that lined the streets, hear the sounds, and feel the brush of the crowds against my shoulders again. It was as if I had never left. And then I started reading the story of a miracle, a moment when God came rushing into our day in an obvious intervention. I was shocked as I read it—because it was like I was reading it for the first time. And then I got to the end, where I had written my testimony and then this line: "I will never forget this experience." But I had.

It is amazing how quickly we can forget how good God has been, the times He has come into our story, the breathtaking miracles we have seen or been a part of. I can hear Nephi asking me the same question he asked his brothers: How is it that ye have forgotten?

God has been and will always be so good. That is certain. The question is, how will we remember it? —DB

Reflect and Respond

What can you do to make sure you do not forget the good things God is doing in your story?

Your favorite
scripture in
1 Nephi 7

1 NEPHI 8:30

And they did press their way forward, continually holding fast to the rod of iron, **until they came forth and fell down** and partook of the fruit of the tree.

Usually, when you get to a tree to pick fruit, you reach up. But in this dream story, there is a group of people who fall down when they get to the tree. Why would they do that? We learn in a later chapter that the tree in the vision represents Jesus Christ—God's greatest manifestation of love to the world. The fruit on the tree represents the gifts of His atoning sacrifice—gifts like forgiveness, strength, peace, and reassurance. So, in the vision, the group that stays is symbolically falling down at the feet of Jesus and receiving His gifts of grace.

With all the reunions I have seen or been a part of, I have never fallen down when I have met someone. I missed my mom terribly when I was a full-time missionary, but even when I saw her at the airport after two long years, although I ran, and cried, and squeezed tight, I didn't fall down. There is something quite different going on in this moment at the tree.

What do you think the people were feeling that would cause this kind of reaction? What did they know about the Savior, and what had they experienced in their lives that caused these feelings and this reaction? Gratitude. Love. Reverence. The type of experiences that caused them to fall on their knees and never forget. —DB

Reflect and Respond

Are you having significant one-on-one experiences with Jesus Christ? Which of those experiences would cause you to fall down at His feet?

Your favorite scripture in 1 Nephi 8

1 NEPHI 9:6

But **the Lord knoweth all things from the beginning**: wherefore, he prepareth a way to accomplish all his works among the children of men; for behold, he hath all power unto the fulfilling of all his words.

If only we could see the end, how it all works out. It would be so much easier. But the majority of our lives are spent in the middle moments, in the working out of it all. Our prayers are filled to overflowing with pleading, Heavenly Father bless this, and send this, and make this happen. We are impatient at times. We lose faith. We wonder how things will turn out.

In the frantic moments, when fear and doubt chase away hope and faith, I turn to this verse. The Lord knows all things, He prepares a way to accomplish his work, He has all power, and thus it is. It is so simple, I almost can't comprehend it. Every time I read it, I take a deep breath, I lean into peace, and I believe.

The Lord knows what to do. He can accomplish what we can't. But it will happen in His own time and in His own way. Our job is to trust that He is working within our waiting, that He has not forgotten us. That He not only knows what to do but will accomplish it.

Lately my prayers have changed. Instead of pleading, *Lord, what should I do?* I say instead, *Lord, you know what to do, and I trust you.* Then I wait for the inspiration that comes in peaceful moments. With time. —EBF

Reflect and Respond

How can you learn to be more patient with the Lord? What would increase your trust that He knows what to do?

Your favorite scripture in 1 Nephi 9

1 NEPHI 10:17

I, Nephi, was desirous **also that I might see, and hear, and know** of these things, by the power of the Holy Ghost, which is the gift of God unto all those who diligently seek him.

I can still remember how disappointing it was to sit with my grandma on the bench while I watched the roller-coaster cars click up the first big hill filled with the bigger kids. The screams were like daggers as they came flying through and around the two big loops. The worst of all was when they came running down the ramp exchanging laughs and congratulatory comments: "That was awesome!" and "Let's go again." I could try going up to the line with them, but I would still be turned away for being just an inch too short. Even with the extra socks I stuffed in my shoes.

There are times when I still feel like this, when I want to experience something that is just out of my reach. I don't want to hear about it—I want to see it for myself. I want to experience it!

This was Nephi's desire too. When he heard what the Lord had shown his father, he was not content to sit on the sidelines. He wanted to see, hear, and know for himself. And the beautiful thing is—he could! The Lord hasn't reserved visions and revelations and spiritual experiences for prophets only. They are gifts for anyone who diligently seeks Him. The Lord has so many thrilling experiences in store for those who want them. No extra socks needed. —DB

Reflect and Respond
What do you wish you could see, or hear, or know for yourself?

Your favorite scripture in 1 Nephi 10

1 NEPHI 11:17

And I said unto him: **I know that he loveth his children**;
nevertheless, I do not know the meaning of all things.

Sometimes the kids come home from school near Mother's Day or Father's Day with little questionnaires about their parents that their teachers had them fill out at school. The teachers ask questions like how old we are, what our childhoods were like, and our favorite things. The kids answer without any help. These papers are always hilarious to read, except that when I am finished, I am convinced that my child is spending half of his or her life with some other person I don't know about. One of my favorites was when the question said, "What is their favorite thing to do?" Answer: "Tell me to clean my room." I am glad my kids think that is what I find most enjoyable about life.

One day they might actually learn my favorite ice-cream flavor, my favorite childhood memory, and how much I legitimately weigh, but until then, there is really only one thing I want them to know—that I unequivocally and indisputably adore them. That I love them to the moon. That's it. That's what I need them to know.

Nephi got asked questions from an angel about the Lord. Some of them he didn't know the answer to. But he knew one thing—that the Lord loves His children. And that made all the "I don't knows" okay for the time being. I am certain if God had one thing he wanted to be sure Nephi knew, it would be that. That He unequivocally and indisputably adored him. That He loved him to the moon. Everything else he could figure out later. —DB

Reflect and Respond

Have you discovered the truth about your relationship with the Lord—that He adores you? When is the last time you felt that?

Your favorite
scripture in
1 Nephi 11

1 NEPHI 12:9

And he said unto me: **Thou rememberest the twelve apostles** of the Lamb?

It was a hard season. My son Josh had just been diagnosed with diabetes at the age of three. My days were spent chasing him around the house, pinning him down, and either poking his fingers to test his blood or giving him a shot so he could eat. He wondered why I didn't do that to any of the other kids. There were moments when he hated me. This was not the mother I wanted to be, not the mother I had planned to be. My sleepless nights were filled with worries of low blood sugars and seizures. It was a dark time.

Five months after Josh was diagnosed, Elder Jeffrey R. Holland stood up to speak at general conference. I remember his words as if he spoke them yesterday: "I say to mothers collectively, in the name of the Lord, you are magnificent. You are doing terrifically well. . . . You will be magnified, compensated, made more than you are and better than you have ever been . . . however feeble you may sometimes feel that to be" ("Because She Is a Mother," *Ensign*, May 2017).

I sat in front of the television set in our family room and wept unabashedly. It was as if Elder Holland were speaking directly to me. If you were to ask me about a moment that I remember with one of the twelve Apostles of the Lamb, this would be one of the first that would come to mind. This moment changed my perspective of motherhood; I daresay it changed my life.

Do you have a moment like this? —EBF

Reflect and Respond

Reflect on personal experiences you have had with an Apostle of the Lord, in person or in a talk that profoundly affected your heart.

Your favorite scripture in 1 Nephi 12

1 NEPHI 13:34

I will be merciful unto the Gentiles in that day, insomuch that I will
bring forth unto them, in mine own power, much of my gospel,
which shall be plain and precious, saith the Lamb.

Up on the top shelf of my closet is a metal box that my grandparents gave me on my eighth birthday. They told me it was for my treasures. Today it is almost impossible to close that box because it is overflowing with my special things. If thieves broke into my house, they wouldn't find anything valuable in there—there is a letter from my grandpa, a red beaded necklace, a bent picture that I could look at over and over again, and a whole bunch of rocks from around the world. There is a little sandstone one that I am particularly fond of. The treasures don't look like much at first—pretty simple—but if they were ever lost, I would be devastated. They mean so much to me, and if I told you the story behind each trinket you would know why I value them so much more than gold.

Over 2,600 years ago, the Lord showed Nephi a vision of a day when He would send treasure to the world. A day of restoration. A day that you and I live in. He promised He would reveal truths that were plain and precious. Treasured truths. Truths that at one time were lost, but then returned. Truths that might appear simple at first, but that, when understood, would lead a heart to overflowing. The Book of Mormon was written on golden plates, but the words that were engraved on those plates had all the value. These truths are precious. Nothing can compare. Not even that little sandstone I'm so fond of. —DB

Reflect and Respond

What is it about the gospel that is plain and precious to you? What are some of your treasured truths?

Your favorite
scripture in
1 Nephi 13

1 NEPHI 14:14

And they were **armed with righteousness and with the power of God** in great glory.

In the book of Revelation, we read of the mark of the beast found in the unbelievers and also the seal in the forehead of the Lord's servants. Many have speculated what that mark might be, or what it would look like. I think of this mark every time I read Nephi's description of those who belong to the abominable church as contrasted with those who are the covenant people of the Lord.

"Behold the formation of a church which is most abominable above all other churches, which slayeth the saints of God, yea, and tortureth them and bindeth them down, and yoketh them with a yoke of iron, and bringeth them down into captivity" (1 Nephi 13:5). Now listen to the description of the other church, "And it came to pass that I, Nephi, beheld the power of the Lamb of God, that it descended upon the saints of the church of the Lamb, and upon the covenant people of the Lord, . . . and they were armed with righteousness and with the power of God in great glory" (1 Nephi 14:14). The difference between the two churches is striking.

We live in a time of turmoil; it is a time of choosing. Some question, others doubt. There is confusion all around. Do you find it interesting that Nephi's simple definitions of good and evil 600 years before Jesus came are just as relevant to those of us living today? One binds, yokes, and brings others down; the other arms with righteousness and God's own power. Each church leaves its mark, and we are given the opportunity to choose. Power over captivity. Light over darkness. Good over evil. —EBF

Reflect and Respond

How have you felt yourself being armed with righteousness? When have you experienced God's own power? What have you learned?

Your favorite scripture in 1 Nephi 14

1 NEPHI 15:8

And I said unto them: **Have ye inquired of the Lord?**

"Come with us!" My friends were planning a super fun trip and I wanted to join them. But instead of asking my parents, I just made up an excuse of why I couldn't go. I was so certain the answer would be no that it wasn't even worth asking. I don't know why asking for things has always been so difficult for me. It doesn't matter what it is—favors, permission, help—it's all the same. I just never ask, and in the case of this trip, it meant I never went.

There is something so vulnerable about asking for something. You have to show your hopes and desires and what you really want. You risk being disappointed or let down. You have to learn why your ideas might not be the best ideas. It's an emotional investment, and investments are always risky. But when you invest nothing, you receive nothing.

Laman and Lemuel heard their father's dream and the teachings the Lord gave him and started asking Nephi curious questions about them. Nephi told them they were asking the wrong person. "Have you asked God?" Their response sounds like something I might say, "The Lord maketh no such thing known unto us" (1 Nephi 15:9). In other words, *He will probably say no.*

But what if He said yes? He did for Nephi. He did for Lehi. What would He have said or given if they would have simply asked? What would they have learned about Him or about themselves? Instead, the two older brothers complained about their journey because "they knew not the dealings of that God who had created them" (1 Nephi 2:12). They made assumptions about Him. They didn't know who He really was. They never experienced life with Him. All because they never asked. —DB

Reflect and Respond

Is there something you are holding back from inquiring of the Lord?

Your favorite scripture in 1 Nephi 15

1 NEPHI 16:29

*…and it was written and changed from time to time, **according to the faith and diligence** which we gave unto it.*

Maybe you seek for understanding. Perhaps you are looking for direction. Are there concerns in your life that have led you to seek for the voice of the Lord? This chapter in the Book of Mormon contains powerful words of advice: if we want to be led into the most fertile parts of the wilderness places in our life, we must follow the instructions of the Lord. Lehi and Nephi used the Liahona for help in knowing what to do. In our life, we turn to the Spirit.

There are several verses in this chapter that increase our understanding of the Liahona—it led into the more fertile parts of the wilderness, it gave understanding, and it changed from time to time (see 1 Nephi 16:16, 29).

The same is true about the Spirit. It leads us, it gives understanding, and the way we hear and respond to the Spirit can change from time to time. The instruction for obtaining this direction and understanding is simple. First, like Nephi and Lehi, we must inquire. Second, we must have faith and diligence and heed His words, which will increase our capacity to hear the Spirit. Last, we must go forth unto the top of the mountain. For us, this might look like standing in holy places, including our homes, our churches, and our temples. Standing in holy places will also increase our ability to hear the whisperings of the Spirit. Besides advice, Nephi also gives us a caution. Anger, murmuring, and complaining will hinder our ability to hear the Lord the same way it prevented the Liahona from working for Lehi's family. The Lord will lead us into fruitful places, but we must give faith and diligence to listening to the Spirit. —EBF

Reflect and Respond

What are you doing to increase your ability to hear the Spirit? What are you doing that might hinder the Spirit from working in your life?

Your favorite scripture in 1 Nephi 16

1 NEPHI 17:21

Behold, these many years we have suffered in the wilderness,
which time we might have enjoyed our possessions and the land
of our inheritance; yea, **and we might have been happy**.

When our oldest boys were little, we went to McDonald's one day, and one of my son's Happy Meal toys broke because he twisted it too hard. It made him so mad, he took his younger brother's toy, broke it, and threw the pieces on the ground. The younger, a little surprised, looked at those pieces on the ground for a moment, then bent down and picked them up. He looked up, and I saw a twinkle in his eyes as he held up the pieces in absolute delight and announced in celebration, "Two!"

One boy saw broken. Another saw a blessing.

As Laman and Lemuel traveled through the wilderness with their family, they often complained about their circumstances, their unknown future, their hardships, and the life they could have had back home. Hot desert, hurt feet, and horrible food.

Nephi, writing of the exact same journey, celebrated how "great were the blessings of the Lord upon us, that while we did live upon raw meat in the wilderness, our women . . . began to bear their journeyings without murmuring" (1 Nephi 17:2). Usually, living off raw meat is not counted as a blessing. But that was how Nephi saw it. His older brothers saw trial, and he saw triumph. They felt failure, and Nephi felt faith. One saw broken, and the other a blessing. What helped Nephi make the journey without murmuring is that He saw God in the wilderness. And that meant happiness wasn't something he could have had but didn't; he discovered it right there. —DB

Reflect and Respond

What life circumstances and situations can you look at right now through this same lens? Do you see God in your wilderness?

Your favorite
scripture in
1 Nephi 17

1 NEPHI 18:3

And I, Nephi, did go into the mount oft, and I did pray oft unto the Lord; wherefore the Lord **showed unto me great things**.

The repetition of certain phrases in scripture helps us to understand when we are seeing an important concept. *Great things* is one of those phrases. It is repeated more than sixty times and can be found in every volume of scripture. It is used to describe what God can do, what man can do with God, and what God has in store in days to come.

Often, when the scriptures talk about the great things, it is an invitation for us to do something we have never done before so God can take us to a place we've never been before. The phrase *great things* leads us to think of miraculous moments, unexpected outcomes, and unlikely destinations.

My fourth pregnancy was complicated. I went into labor at seventeen weeks and spent six months on complete bed rest. When Grace was born, the doctor called her a miracle baby. We had experienced a miraculous moment. A great thing. Several weeks after we returned home from the hospital, my dad came over to visit. He encouraged me to write down all the miracles we had experienced over those six months. I remember telling him that I wouldn't forget any of them—they had left a profound impression on my heart— but I followed his advice anyway. When Grace turned eighteen, I found the journal where I had written those memories down. I hadn't read those words since I wrote them. My dad was right; I had forgotten so many of the details, so many of the great things. I would never have remembered if I hadn't written them down. It made me wonder how many great things I have forgotten. —EBF

Reflect and Respond

Write down the great things the Lord is doing in your life. Add to the list all day. What do you learn about the Lord?

Your favorite scripture in 1 Nephi 18

1 NEPHI 19:24

Hear ye the words of the prophet, which were written unto all the house of Israel, and liken them unto yourselves, **that ye may have hope as well as your brethren** ... for after this manner has the prophet written.

I once stood in a hospital room that had several people in it. There were doctors, nurses, family members, the patient in the bed, and then there was me. They were all trying to make some difficult decisions about what to do next. As I looked at those people and listened to them talk, I thought about the different role that each person played. The nurses were there to care; the doctors were there to diagnose, prescribe, and offer medical advice. Some family members were there to ask for more information, and some were there to make decisions.

Then there was me. I thought about it as I drove home from the hospital. What was my job? It dawned on me in a whisper to my heart: "Your job is to speak hope." As the days went on, I took on that job seriously. I reminded everyone of miracles and what could be. I brought up reasons to believe. I tried to make an invisible God's hand visible to those who were there. My job was to breathe out hope.

Nephi taught that others wrote scripture for this same reason. One of the prophets he was fond of quoting was Isaiah. What was his job in writing? Hope. He wrote that those who read "may have hope." That they might have something to believe. That they might see the hand of the Lord and His miracles working in their lives. That they might remember that they worship a God of "good things to come" (Hebrews 9:11). This might be the central purpose of all of scripture: to speak hope. —DB

Reflect and Respond

What can you have hope in today? How can you breathe that hope into situations around you right now?

Your favorite scripture in 1 Nephi 19

1 NEPHI 20:10

For, behold, **I have refined thee**,
I have chosen thee in the furnace of affliction.

Francis Webster was a pioneer who traveled with the Martin handcart company. He had enough money to have made the crossing in a more expensive covered wagon, but he chose to purchase a simple handcart for his family, and with his remaining money he purchased handcarts for other families who had no way to cross the plains. In speaking of the journey, he once said, "Was I sorry that I chose to come by handcart? No! Neither then nor any minute of my life since. The price we paid to become acquainted with God was a privilege to pay, and I am thankful that I was privileged to come in the Martin Handcart Company" (*Relief Society Magazine,* January 1948, 8).

I think about the storms he faced, the weariness from illness, the exposure and starvation, and I can't help but wonder if there were days he wished he had taken the covered wagon. I am reminded of the trials of my own life, things I wish we had never had to pass through, sorrow and sadness and discouragement that left us weary and worn through. I look back at those moments and know what Francis Webster was describing. Those are the moments when I came to know the Lord. Those moments are precious to me. I would not give them up for anything.

President James E. Faust once wrote: "Here, then, is a great truth. In the pain, the agony, and the heroic endeavors of life, we pass through a refiner's fire, and the insignificant and the unimportant in our lives can melt away like dross and make our faith bright, intact, and strong. . . . It is part of the purging toll exacted of some to become acquainted with God" ("Refined in Our Trials," *Ensign,* February 2006). —EBF

Reflect and Respond

Consider your refining moments. What did you learn about the Lord during each of those trials?

Your favorite scripture in 1 Nephi 20

1 NEPHI 21:16

Behold, **I have graven thee upon the palms of my hands**; thy walls are continually before me.

Before this verse, Isaiah asked if a mother could ever forget her little baby. Is that even possible?

A few years ago, my friends told me a story of loading all their kids into the car to head to Grandma's house. The dad carried their newborn baby out in the car seat and set it up on the roof of the car while he buckled in the rest of the kids. After wrestling to get them all in their spots, he shut the door, hopped into the driver's seat, and started the car, forgetting about the baby.

They pulled out of their driveway and stopped at the stop sign that was just at the corner of their street when his wife looked up in horror and yelled, "The baby!" He quickly put the car in park, and they both flew out of their seat belts, got out, and looked up to find the car seat gently rocking back and forth with an oblivious and happy baby cooing in it. The parents exchanged glances. Dad swallowed hard, reached up, got the baby, opened the side door, and clicked the baby in before they started on the rest of their trip in thankful relief and silence.

Can a mother or father forget their newborn baby? *Yes, they may forget, yet will I not forget thee. You are engraved in the palms of my hands.* The truth is, even parents and dear friends can fail us in our lives—but not Jesus. After all that He has done for us—including and especially dying for us on Calvary's cross—the Lord will never be able to forget us. We are always before Him. And He will always be for us. —DB

Reflect and Respond

How does it make you feel to know that you are always in the hands and heart of a God who loves you so fully?

Your favorite scripture in 1 Nephi 21

1 NEPHI 22:12

...and they shall know that the Lord is **their Savior and their Redeemer**, the Mighty One of Israel.

I was once talking to a Jewish friend about my desire to learn Hebrew. He knew my love of the scriptures and so he responded enthusiastically, "You really do want to know Hebrew! But do you know why?" I thought I did, but I could tell by the sparkle in his eyes that there was something I was missing, so I asked him to tell me why *he* thought *I* wanted to learn Hebrew. He responded with these words of advice: "When you read a scripture in English you think every word has one meaning, and your interpretation comes from that one meaning. In Hebrew every word has several meanings. Some have up to twenty. When I read a word in scripture I think about every meaning of the word, and the verse comes alive for me."

Now, after spending time with my Jewish friend, one of my favorite scripture-study tips is to research the Greek and Hebrew meanings of the words that I want to understand better. The word *Savior* and the word *Redeemer* are two of my favorite examples of this.

The Hebrew word for Savior is *Yasha,* which means to free, to succor, to defend, to deliver, to help, to preserve, and to rescue. The Greek word for save is *sozo,* which means to deliver, protect, heal, preserve, and make whole.

The Hebrew word for redeem is *ga'al,* to deliver in any wise, and *padah,* to preserve, deliver, rescue, surely and by any means (see *The New Strong's Expanded Exhaustive Concordance of the Bible,* 2001).

The extra understanding helped me to recognize that Jesus Christ will deliver, help, rescue, heal, and make whole, surely and by any means. The knowledge has made the names *Savior* and *Redeemer* more sacred to me. —EBF

Reflect and Respond

Try replacing the words Savior *and* Redeemer *with one of their synonyms. How does it help you better understand that scripture?*

Your favorite scripture in 1 Nephi 22

2 NEPHI 1:30

I know that **thou art a true friend** unto my son, Nephi, forever.

A few years ago, one of my dearest friends passed away early in life after a courageous battle with bone cancer. In one of those tender moments in the days before he died, we had a chance to sit together on his bed and relive and laugh about all our memories from growing up. I never get tired of telling those stories! As part of that conversation, I stopped all the laughing for a minute to be serious and tell him how much I loved him and what a good friend he had always been to me. I told him, "If I was ever with you, I knew I wouldn't be in trouble." He looked back at me and said, "I can't say the same about you! But I loved every minute!" I was always the mischievous one.

Think of the wild adventures Nephi and Zoram had together. Leaving the house of Laban knowing they would never return to Jerusalem, camping in the wilderness, building a boat, and crossing the stormy sea. They would have had some stories! When Lehi died, he must have sensed that the troubles were not over for them. I love thinking about how comforted he must have been to know that Nephi would not face all those times ahead alone. He would have Zoram, a true friend forever, someone who would protect him, defend him, and remind him about the goodness of God. And hopefully someone who would keep him out of trouble. A friend forever is a friend who has his eyes set on the future, who sees your potential and eternal perspective. This is what makes Jesus Christ the truest friend of all. He sees all in you, believes all that is good, hopes all the best to come, and is there to endure it all by your side. —DB

Reflect and Respond

Who do you know who is a true friend forever to you? How are you living as a true friend to someone else?

Your favorite scripture in 2 Nephi 1

2 NEPHI 2:30

And I have chosen the good part.

One afternoon my boys were arguing in the basement over a toy pirate ship. I leaned over the banister and yelled, "Caleb, choose the right!" Caleb must have been four years old at the time, and because he was the oldest, I expected him to figure it out. I remember how he came and stood at the bottom of the stairs to look up at me, his big blue eyes pleading for understanding. "I am, Mom," he said, trying to help me understand the situation, "but Josh is on the left!" I'm not going to lie, I laughed so hard.

Life is about choosing. Every day we are faced with decisions about how to act and what to do. If we ever want a lesson on this process, the second chapter of 2 Nephi is filled with advice about making choices and acting for ourselves. It contains words such as *act, choose, look, hearken,* and *be faithful.* But it also is filled with words such as *joy* and *happiness.* My favorite part of this chapter is found in the very last verse. Lehi is about to die. He is giving advice to each of his children, one by one. It is Jacob's turn, and Lehi is giving him counsel, expecting him to figure it out, helping him to know what to do. He ends the conversation with six simple words, "I have chosen the good part." It is such good advice. We can't help but be reminded of another home with similar instruction. Instead of a father and a son, it is two sisters learning from the Lord. He reminds both of them also to choose the good part, for it shall not be taken away (see Luke 10:42).

What is the good part? Sitting at the feet of the Lord. Learning to act for ourselves. Discovering happiness. Doing good. Choosing liberty and eternal life. Looking to the great mediator. Being faithful. And so much more. —EBF

Reflect and Respond
How could you choose the good part today?

Your favorite scripture in 2 Nephi 2

2 NEPHI 3:19

And the words which he shall write shall be the words which are
expedient in my wisdom should go forth . . . **for I know their faith**.

I love this multigenerational chapter from the Book of Mormon. It is the story of a father, Lehi, telling his son about the writings of his ancestor Joseph of Egypt. Interestingly, Joseph of Egypt was prophesying about the future prophet Joseph Smith, who would be an instrument in bringing forth these ancient conversations in our day.

It is so brilliant to then hear the Lord say of the whole tapestry, "I know their faith." He knows the sacrifice and the yearning and the striving of all of these generations of people. They scribbled on parchment or etched words into metal to pass down the story of God. The words went forth. The Lord made sure of it. Thousands of years later, they would come out of the ground and be passed down through time as a way to strengthen future generations, and as a way for God to honor those who trusted Him enough to write.

This is the story of scripture. And it continues from pulpits, front porches, and even at bedtimes with parents.

My friend was asked one day after seminary if he wanted to write down his testimony in the inside front cover of a Book of Mormon. He took the time to do it and figured that was the end of it. Then, years later, he received a letter from a stranger from the Middle East who had come across the book, read his witness, taken his challenge, and come to know the truth about God. The Lord saw my friend's faith and let his front-cover words go forth, just like the rest of the words in the book, across an ocean and into the heart of a new generation of people. —DB

Reflect and Respond

What can you do to continue to send the word of God forth into the hearts of the people you know—and even those you might not?

Your favorite
scripture in
2 Nephi 3

2 NEPHI 4:19

Nevertheless, I know in whom I have trusted.

My husband picked Garett up off the curb with all of his belongings when he was eighteen years old, and thus began an eighteen-month journey to turn his life around. Our family had strict rules, but they were all meant to keep him safe. One weekend night he wanted to go out with friends. I was a little bit worried about the people and the situation. I just didn't feel good about it. So I asked if he could choose to do something else. "Why don't you trust me?" was his immediate response. The Spirit prompted my reply, "Why don't you trust *me*? Have I ever done anything that wasn't for your good?" His defiant eyes softened as he thought about the question, and then he shook his head.

Like Garett, I have questioned the Lord. I have wondered if He has forgotten me. I have felt the doubt that comes when a prayer goes unanswered time after time. I wonder how often the Lord wants to whisper that same question to me: *Why don't you trust Me? Have I ever done anything that wasn't for your good?*

I remember the pain Nephi had been through when I read 2 Nephi 4. The loss of his father, the years of struggle, the anger of his brothers. I love how Nephi turned the questions of his heart into courage to move forward by describing what he had learned of the Lord through the struggle: *He has filled me with his love, confounded my enemies, heard my cries, given me knowledge, sent angels to minister to me, carried me on the wings of his Spirit, and caused me to see great things* (see 2 Nephi 4:21–26).

Through it all, the Lord had given him reason to trust, and Nephi declared that he would trust in Him forever (see 2 Nephi 4:34). —EBF

Reflect and Respond
How has the Lord taught you to trust?

Your favorite scripture in 2 Nephi 4

2 NEPHI 5:27

**And it came to pass that we lived
after the manner of happiness.**

Somewhere in the middle of downtown Tijuana, Mexico, there is a little village of people who live in the garbage dump. Their houses are made of corrugated sheet metal, dirt floors, and rotting planks of wood, with tattered bedsheets for front doors. Down on the bottom level of the dump is a little church with a ministry to serve breakfast each morning to the families who call that place home. We visited there a few years ago and made breakfast, played Duck-Duck-Goose on the porch with the kids, and carried baskets full of needed supplies up the trash mountain to the homes of our new friends. We loved each other, prayed for each other, and promised to remember each other.

As we drove through the border leaving Mexico, I asked each of the kids what they were bringing home with them. I wasn't talking about the new T-shirts and blankets they had bought at the market, but the lessons they wanted to bring home. My oldest said something I'll never forget. He said, "Before I came here, I didn't know that you could find happiness and God in the middle of a garbage dump. But now I know you can."

There is a lot we can learn from 2 Nephi 5 about what it means to live after the manner of happiness. Whatever other principles you discover, perhaps one you will notice is the same one my son did. You can find happiness anywhere. And you can find God anywhere. And those go hand in hand. —DB

Reflect and Respond

*When have you lived after the manner of happiness? Is there
something you remember from that time that you can repeat today?*

Your favorite
scripture in
2 Nephi 5

2 NEPHI 6:7

And thou shalt know that I am the Lord; **for they shall not be ashamed that wait for me**.

Many years ago, Israel waited for a king to deliver her from her oppressor. The people talked about it, planned for it, and waited. One day, He came—not on a white horse with a sword prepared to defeat the Roman Empire, but on a gray donkey prepared to overcome bondage with a cross. It was so unexpected, many people in Jerusalem missed the sign of deliverance.

For those who missed that sign, I wonder if the continued rule of Rome left them discouraged as they questioned if their Savior would ever come. But those who knew understood that the power of deliverance would overcome more than just the Roman Empire; it would overcome death, and sin, and hell. These believers knew that the man on the gray donkey was the Lord they had waited for.

One day He will come again.

Just like before, many people question if that day will ever come. But when He comes, people will not be able to miss the sign of His coming. This time He will manifest himself in power and great glory. Enemies will be destroyed. At the Second Coming, everyone will know that He is the Lord, the Savior, and the Redeemer, "for the Mighty God shall deliver his covenant people" (2 Nephi 6:17).

And so, we wait.

With courage. With hope. With assurance. —EBF

Reflect and Respond

What does it look like to wait with hope and assurance? How might those two words define your actions during the waiting?

Your favorite scripture in 2 Nephi 6

2 NEPHI 7:4

**When you are weary he
waketh morning by morning.**

I once had a conversation with a good friend who struggles with depression. He explained how debilitating it was, especially in the mornings. I knew exactly what he was talking about. I have been through bouts of depression myself.

We talked about the tools we both rely on during particularly hard days: going out into the sunshine, taking deep breaths, focusing our thoughts on something we are passionate about, and working with professionals who understand how to fight depression better than we could on our own. "But what do you do in the mornings?" my friend asked. "What do you do when you can't get out of bed?"

Immediately a verse of scripture came to mind.

In those first days of depression, mornings were hard for me. I felt weary, and the day hadn't even begun. But I also felt lonely and hopeless. Then, one day, I stumbled upon this scripture, "When you are weary he waketh morning by morning" (2 Nephi 7:4). The truth of it settled on my heart. I wasn't alone. The Lord was already awake, no matter what time the morning started for me. And it didn't matter how many mornings I woke up weary, He would be there morning by morning to meet me.

"I learned to begin my weary mornings in conversation with Him," I told my friend. "We would talk through the weariness, I would pray for strength, and His Spirit would fill me. When you are weary in the morning, turn to Him."

Sometimes a verse of scripture becomes a lifeline during the hard moments of life. For me, this scripture is one of those. —EBF

Reflect and Respond

*Next time you are having a hard morning, try sharing your
weariness with Him.*

Your favorite
scripture in
2 Nephi 7

2 NEPHI 8:12

I am he; yea, I am he that comforteth you.

I remember the first time I needed to make a résumé for a job application. Because of my lack of experience and skills at the time, I padded my résumé with exaggerations and irrelevant information. It may or may not have included the line "I'm a great person to be around" as one of my skill sets. I didn't get the job.

What if the Lord created a résumé? What would be on it? If I needed to choose a chapter from the scriptures that would be a fitting résumé for Him, it might be 2 Nephi 8. As you move through the chapter, you find that the God of Israel is one who:

Dried the sea

Wounded the dragon

Comforted Israel

Planted the heavens

Laid the foundation of the earth

Isn't this who you are? the prophet Isaiah asked. "I am he," He replied. "I am the Lord thy God" (2 Nephi 8:12, 15).

At first glance, it seems like He might be trying to impress, but He doesn't need to. He is God. He is not applying for the position. He already has it. Instead, the Lord is trying to convince Israel to trust Him, to allow Him not just to be Lord and God but to be *their* Lord and God. Imagine leaning on and trusting the God who dries seas, wounds dragons, and lays the foundation of the earth. This is who He is.

And after describing who He is, the Lord ends by giving us a line for our own résumés. "I am the Lord thy God, . . . [and] thou art my people" (2 Nephi 8:15, 16). —DB

Reflect and Respond

If you were to add a line to the Lord's "résumé," what would you add?

Your favorite scripture in 2 Nephi 8

2 NEPHI 9:41

And **the keeper of the gate** is the Holy One of Israel;
and he employeth no servant there.

Hundreds of years ago there was a practice known to all the shepherds in Jerusalem. It had to do with the keeper of the gate. It was the shepherd's responsibility to care for his little flock of sheep night and day. He did not sit at a fenced-in field and keep an eye on them; he walked the land with them. He would lead them to fresh water, and when the sun beat down he would find a tree under which they could settle into the shade. He stayed away from dangerous places and kept his eye out for enemies. When he ran out of food or needed supplies, he would come into town to the market.

A flock of sheep is not safe on the streets of a market, so the shepherd would drop them off to a fenced-in pen where they would be safe until he returned. In every place of safekeeping there was an experienced shepherd who was known as the keeper of the gate. He was there when you dropped the sheep off, and you could trust that he would be there when you returned. He knew each shepherd who dropped off his sheep—how he knew the names of each lamb, how they followed him. This shepherd's job was safekeeping, watchcare, and protection. He took this job seriously; he would never employ a servant to take his place.

I think of this every time I read this verse. The Holy One of Israel keeps the gate. He knows our names. He provides safekeeping, watchcare, and protection. He is always there.

Always. —EBF

Reflect and Respond

How does knowing that the Holy One of Israel is the keeper of the gate bring you peace?

Your favorite
scripture in
2 Nephi 9

2 NEPHI 10:20

Seeing that our merciful God has given us so great knowledge concerning these things, let us remember him, and lay aside our sins, and **not hang down our heads**, for we are not cast off.

The family I grew up in and the family I am raising all love sports, which means I have been to lots of games that ended with jumps, hollers, and celebrations. I have also been to several games that ended with tears, mumbled responses, and heads that hung down. Of all the sports, I think baseball is the toughest. Even though it is a team sport, there is an individual aspect to it. There you are, one-on-one at the plate, the pitcher and the batter, and everyone is looking at you! One pitch could make you a hero or cost your team the game. I cannot think of many things harder than walking back to the dugout after the third strike on the third out. It is almost impossible to not hang your head down in a moment like that.

In baseball, after too many at bats like that, you could get benched. In the major leagues, you could be cut from the team. Those are real possibilities. But not in the game of life. Not with a God like the one we worship. I love Jacob's reminder in this verse: a reminder of a merciful God. One who allows us to keep our chins up even after our mistakes. One who lets us set those sins aside. You and I are never off the team. We have never gone too far to return. "Let us remember Him," Jacob said. A God who refuses to bench us, cast us off, or hold us to a "three strikes you're out" policy. A God who doesn't want us to hang our heads. —DB

Reflect and Respond

When you are tempted to hang your head down in regret or shame, what could you remember about our God to give you hope?

Your favorite scripture in 2 Nephi 10

2 NEPHI 11:5

My soul delighteth in his grace.

Have you ever wondered what grace is? Some describe it as favor or goodwill. The Bible Dictionary defines it as a divine means of help or strength, an enabling power that comes through the mercy and love of the Father and the Son. I have felt this enabling strength, this divine help. Most often it comes in my moments of weakness.

I remember the woman with the issue of blood. I read how she struggled with her illness for twelve years, how it left her unclean, untouchable. I imagine her longing to be made whole. I know those moments. Weariness. Loneliness. The struggle that overwhelms day after day. My thoughts often turn to her touching His robe. The reaching out. The last resort. In the Savior's reply a great lesson is taught: "Somebody hath touched me: for I perceive that virtue is gone out of me" (Luke 8:46). The Greek word for *virtue* here is *dunamis,* meaning "miraculous power or strength." Both are words that testify of grace.

Perhaps this story is what grace looks like: a divine means of help or strength, an enabling power that comes through the mercy and love of the Son to heal, to make one whole.

Stories like this remind us of the power of His grace, and then our souls can't help but delight in His grace. —EBF

Reflect and Respond

How many years have you struggled with something? Where could you use divine help and grace? How could you reach for the Lord?

Your favorite scripture in 2 Nephi 11

2 NEPHI 12:5

O house of Jacob, come ye and let us **walk in the light of the Lord**;
yea, come, for ye have all gone astray, every one to his wicked ways.

Every time I read this verse, I think it is a no-brainer—an easy yes. It is an invitation to be a part of three things I love—people, light, and Jesus.

The prophet Isaiah is asking the house of Jacob (or children of Israel) to walk with him in the light of the Lord. He is not giving directions of where to go, but he is inviting us to come along where he is already going. "Let us walk in the light," he says. I cannot think of any reason I wouldn't want to go. What great company! A walk is nice—but a walk with a friend wins for me every time.

And this walk is not just anywhere, but a walk in the light of the Lord. There is not much advantage to darkness. It is scary, discouraging, and limiting. It is harder to see, colder, and there is so much you can't do. Light is warm and encouraging. And this light, the light of the Lord, beams down with rays of love, hope, and grace. On this walk, you can turn your face up to the light of the Son and be warmed by His presence.

When the Lord or His prophets invite us to turn from our wicked ways, those are always invitations to a better way. A better walk of life. Out of the darkness. Out of loneliness. Into the companionship and light of His way. —DB

Reflect and Respond

If you were to invite someone to join you on a walk in the light and ways of the Lord, how would you describe what it is like?

Your favorite scripture in 2 Nephi 12

2 NEPHI 13:8

For Jerusalem is ruined, and Judah is fallen, **because their tongues and their doings** have been against the Lord.

What if someone used words like this to describe your life?

Behave proudly	Oppressed	Caused to err
Fallen	Desolate	Grind the faces
Destroyed	Beaten to pieces	Mourn
Burning Lament	Ruined	

This is a description of the city of Jerusalem and her people who got into trouble "because their tongues and their doings have been against the Lord." Consider the meaning behind the words *tongue* and *doings*. The scripture invites us to consider what we *say* and what we *do*. This was a group of people who fell because everything they said and did was against the Lord.

What if we were to live the opposite of the words in this verse? What if everything we said and did was *for* the Lord? What would that look like? The Lord has a message for these people as well: "Say unto the righteous that it is well with them; for they shall eat the fruit of their doings" (2 Nephi 13:10).

Our choices come with consequences every time. When we make a bad choice, we experience a bad consequence; when we make a good choice, we experience a good consequence. Our choices can lead to sweetness, beauty, righteousness, and fruit, or they can lead to burning, desolation, oppression, and ruin. The Lord leaves it up to us. He stands up to plead for us, but He won't take away our agency. The choice is ours. —EBF

Reflect and Respond

Take some time to consider whether what you say and do is for the Lord. What are you doing well? What could you do differently?

Your favorite scripture in 2 Nephi 13

2 NEPHI 14:6

...a place of refuge, **and a covert from the storm** and from rain.

Many years ago, I attended a youth activity up a canyon surrounded by high mountains. There was a storm brewing in the valley as we prepared to leave. By the time we arrived at the location and unpacked the camp chairs, we knew we were in trouble. The approaching clouds were dark and heavy, and we could hear the rumbling of thunder. The camp host came to welcome our group and suggested we should consider moving our location. She pointed to a pavilion just down the hillside. We picked up our chairs and began the walk as heavy drops of rain began to fall. We ducked inside and began setting up our chairs just in time for the brunt of the storm to hit.

There were no walls or doors or windows, but there was a huge roof overhead. Instead of roasting marshmallows around a fire, we sat still and watched the storm roll in. It was loud and powerful, flashes of lightning with the deep boom of thunder, rain pouring out of the dark clouds and pattering a constant rhythm on the tin roof. We were in awe of the strength of the storm, and every time the lightning flashed and thunder echoed off the canyon walls, I thought how grateful I was for our shelter. The storm was beautiful only because we knew we were protected.

In the great storms of life, we too can find protection. The Lord has said He will send a pillar of fire by night and a shadow in the daytime from heat. He will provide a place of refuge and a covert from the storm and from rain. It does not matter how intense the storm; He will be there as a defense and a protection.

That is the promise of the Lord. —EBF

Reflect and Respond

When have you experienced the protection of the Lord as the storms of life raged around you?

Your favorite scripture in 2 Nephi 14

2 NEPHI 15:4

What could have been done more
to my vineyard that I have not done in it?

I am not much of a plant person. Plants just do not do well under my care. We once planted a whole garden box full of squash, and every one of those plants died. My neighbor, a longtime farmer, came over and said, "How did you do that? Squash can grow on a driveway." Truthfully, I don't put much time or effort into plants, which is certainly the reason they die.

In 2 Nephi 15, the master of the vineyard explains all the effort he went through to produce a fruitful crop. He planted the grapes in the richest soil and the best conditions. He pulled the rocks out of the ground and planted the premium vines with a tower and fence to surround them with protection and give them a place to thrive. He did everything He could have done, and still the grapes grew small and wild. The vineyard master then lamented, "What could have been done more?" When I read this, I don't care that the plants died. I have no emotional connection. But what if that was your livelihood? What if you went bankrupt if your plants died? It would cause serious heartache.

It got me thinking—what would break my heart to lose? What would break God's heart? Why the emotion about the grapes? It's because they are symbolic of people. It is God's children that He doesn't want to lose. And He will do anything in His power to help them live fruitful, abundant lives. What would you do if it were your child? —DB

Reflect and Respond
What do you see God doing in your life and the lives of those you love to protect and create conditions that would allow you to thrive?

Your favorite scripture in 2 Nephi 15

2 NEPHI 16:8

Whom shall I send, and who will go for us?
Then I said: **Here am I; send me**.

Have you ever had a "turnaround moment" in your life? An experience that is so life changing that it moves you to make different decisions or head in a different direction?

This is the experience Isaiah seemed to have. Isaiah described walking into the presence of the Lord. He saw Him sitting on His throne in the temple surrounded by holy angels. Immediately Isaiah felt uncomfortable being there. "I am undone," he said. "I am a man of unclean lips; and I dwell in the midst of a people of unclean lips." He felt unfit for where he was and who he was. Perhaps he also felt unfit for what the Lord was asking Him to do. His cries of shame and refusal were answered with an angel bringing a hot coal from the altar of the temple and touching it to his lips—purging his sins and iniquity away.

In the temple, the fire on the altar was a symbol of Jesus Christ. Isaiah had a cleansing and personal encounter with the love of the Lord. After this experience, when the voice of the Lord asked whom He could send—who would volunteer to go forth with His message—Isaiah immediately answered, "Send me."

He went from discouraged and ashamed to determined and enthusiastic. And what was his turning point? An experience with the love of Jesus—the burning, purging love of the Lord. It can be the same for each of us. When we feel the power of His love and grace, we are changed. —DB

Reflect and Respond

Have you had a turnaround moment? What did you learn or feel about the Lord that ignited the change?

Your favorite scripture in 2 Nephi 16

_____

_____

2 NEPHI 17:14

Behold, a virgin shall conceive, and shall bear a son,
and shall call his name Immanuel.

Six hundred years before the first Christmas, Isaiah prophesied about the birth of the Lord Jesus and gave him a title, and His name was called *Immanuel.* In Hebrew, this is a word that means "God with us" (Matthew 1:23). As you know from the story, the mighty Jehovah, God of heaven and earth, came down into the world as a baby to be with us. Here in this place. In our stories. He left the comfort of His throne on high to be together with those He loved. And not only did He come to earth, but He came to earth to a poor Nazarene family in a Bethlehem barn.

If the angels had not come to the shepherds who were out in the fields that first Christmas night to tell them where to find the little baby, they probably never would have gone looking for Him in the stable. He was the future King of kings. He belonged in a temple, palace, synagogue, or other holy place. Instead, they would find Him in the meekness and mess of the manger. I can almost hear the shepherds asking the question, "There? In that place?" And the answer is yes—in that place. He decided to come here and live among us—with us.

Where Jesus chooses to be is an indication of who He is. He chose to come to the earth as Immanuel, not to be distant up in the heavens, but to be here, with us, in our messy places. To meet us as we are in our stories. —DB

Reflect and Respond

When have you experienced Jesus as Immanuel? When have you seen Him as a God who is here with us?

Your favorite scripture in 2 Nephi 17

2 NEPHI 18:17

And **I will wait upon the Lord**, . . . and I will look for him.

Have you ever been in the waiting place? It's not the beginning of the trial, and it's long before the miracle comes. It's the place in the middle, when you aren't sure how things are going to turn out.

What are you supposed to do in the waiting?

Once, when I was in the middle of a trial, I began a scripture study of the word *wait*. It was a life-changing experience for me. I had never before noticed how many important lessons are learned in the waiting place. Some of the very best lessons are found in the book of Psalms. Here is one of my favorites: "Wait on the Lord: be of good courage, and he shall strengthen thine heart: wait, I say, on the Lord" (Psalm 27:14).

In 2 Nephi, Isaiah teaches us that part of the waiting includes learning to look for the Lord. It is important counsel. Sometimes waiting makes us wonder if the Lord has forgotten us, if our situation is unimportant to Him, if we even matter. When we look for the Lord in the small things and find Him there, it will remind us that He hasn't forgotten us in the big things. Looking for the Lord is part of what will give us courage and strengthen our hearts in the waiting places of our lives. —EBF

Reflect and Respond

How have you have learned to look for the Lord in a waiting place?

Your favorite scripture in 2 Nephi 18

2 NEPHI 19:3

Thou hast multiplied the nation, and increased the joy—
they joy before thee according to the joy in the harvest,
and as men rejoice when they divide the spoil.

We worship a multiplying God. Think about all the times throughout scripture when you have seen Him take something or someone and make it more. My first thoughts go to a few barley loaves that He used to feed thousands—and there were leftovers! Or fishermen who dropped down their empty nets for a catch and pulled them up bursting and breaking with fish. Whatever we place into His hands, He has the power to make it more. If the Lord can do great things with a single loaf, imagine what He could do with a single life. If He has the power to multiply fishes, imagine what He can increase in each of us.

A few years ago, I stood in a priesthood circle and blessed our baby boy. I thought my joy was full to the brim. Later that evening, my grandpa took me aside and said, "You will not know what the phrase 'joy in your posterity' means until you stand in the circle to bless your great-grandson. The best is yet to come."

Our God is an increasing God. The joy you feel today has a promise from Him of increasing, of multiplying. In Isaiah's words in this verse, it will be like the joy of a harvest or the joy of dividing a spoil: a harvest that is great but started as a tiny seed, and a spoil or prize so big it has to be divided. These are promises of multiplying and increasing joy. Promises of the best that is yet to come. —DB

Reflect and Respond

When have you seen God multiply or increase your capacity or your joy?

Your favorite scripture in 2 Nephi 19

2 NEPHI 20:3

To whom will ye flee for help?

This is a similar question to the one Peter asked Jesus, "Lord, to whom shall we go?" (John 6:68). In times of trouble or trial, when we are weary or defeated, if we are lost or in need of a rescue, to whom will we flee for help? I love the two-word warning given in verse 4 of 2 Nephi 20, "Without me . . ." and then the Lord describes the destruction that will come upon Israel if they don't turn to Him. I can't help but think of what could happen in our lives if we lived the opposite of the warning in that verse. What if we were to live life *with Him*? What if we ran to Him for help, first and always?

A grade-school principal once showed me, because he knew I would love it, the worksheet of a first-grade boy who was learning about prepositions. The paper described a situation, and each student was supposed to fill in the blank with a prepositional phrase such as *in the closet, under the bed,* or *on the dresser.* One of the questions on the worksheet talked about a boy losing his belt and asked where he should look. Instead of choosing one of the prescribed answers, this boy had written an answer of his own: *Jesus will help you.*

I loved that in a time of need, for someone who needed help, Jesus was his first response. He chose to live life with Him.

I want to be like that. —EBF

Reflect and Respond

Consider what it might look like to live life without Christ. What is one way you might live life with *Him today?*

Your favorite scripture in 2 Nephi 20

2 NEPHI 21:2

And the Spirit of the Lord shall rest upon him, **the spirit of wisdom and understanding**, the spirit of counsel and might, the spirit of knowledge and of the fear of the Lord.

In my mind, I imagine so many different people reading these words from Isaiah. I see a mother who doesn't know what to do about her troubled child. A missionary wondering how to help the new family who walked in through the chapel doors. A neighbor who needs courage to love in a way that will be received. A senior in high school deciding which yes is the best yes for college, career, or mission. I see them bowing their heads in prayer. And then, as if they were being crowned by heaven, I imagine the Spirit of the Lord resting upon them—gently and powerfully—endowing them with wisdom, understanding, counsel, knowledge, and might.

There is no handbook that could adequately answer the variety of questions and situations that each of us will face during our journeys. Any given day could be met with a different problem, question, or opportunity that we will not know how to handle. Some advice might be welcomed, appreciated, and needed, but the decisions will still be ours to make. And the forks in our roads will most likely always have more than one destination.

In these times, I hope we remember these words from Isaiah. I hope we remember His promises of the strength, wisdom, and power that can be our guide and companion as we move forward. Our God knows our situations and our futures. In times of frustration or worry or discouragement, His Spirit can rest upon us and tenderly direct our thoughts and paths. He has the capacity and compassion to help. —DB

Reflect and Respond

Where do you need His wisdom, understanding, and might today?

Your favorite scripture in 2 Nephi 21

2 NEPHI 22:5

**Sing unto the Lord;
for he hath done excellent things.**

When my grandmother died, we gathered at her graveside after the funeral. Our whole family was there, but close friends were invited as well. I remember one family in particular. They were from Fiji, where my grandparents had served a mission.

Just before my uncle dedicated the grave, this large family from Fiji stood and made their way up to the front of the group. Reverently and with great emotion they sang a simple song of love and adoration in memory of my grandmother. I still remember their accents and the soothing message of the song sung in their Maori language. The singing was a beautiful expression of their love.

When I read this verse, it reminds me of that moment, and I wonder how often we sing in love and adoration for Him, for the excellent things He has done.

Every Sunday we have the opportunity to gather together and worship. Part of that worship includes the singing of hymns. It is a time for remembering Him and expressing our gratitude through song for what He has done. Sometimes it seems we stumble through the singing, mumbling the words; perhaps we even forget to open the book. What if the whole congregation entered into the singing with the enthusiasm suggested by Isaiah? "Cry out and shout, . . . for great is the Holy One of Israel in the midst of thee" (2 Nephi 22:6).

Perhaps we should try it. —EBF

Reflect and Respond

Try singing the hymns with a little more heartfelt devotion this week. As you sing, consider the excellent things the Lord has done.

Your favorite scripture in 2 Nephi 22

2 NEPHI 23:4

The noise of the multitude in the mountains like as of a great people,
...the Lord of Hosts **mustereth the hosts of the battle**.

Every good battle movie has a scene in which the good guys are surrounded by the enemy—nowhere to go, outnumbered, with a dreaded fate approaching. We hear the sound of soldiers stomping and the drumbeat of war. And then, at that moment when hope and chances run out, reinforcements come. Another army, bigger and stronger than the enemy, runs over the hills to rescue with a battle cry and the belief of victory. My favorite movies are always the ones in which the good guys are saved!

The *Lord of Hosts* is a name for Jesus that means a captain or general of an army. In His case, an army of angels is at His command. An army that outnumbers any enemy we may have to face. An army that has the strength and wisdom and might of heaven. An army that, in the end, wins.

I have never been to war before, but I have seen and been in many battles in my lifetime. Many of them felt like the war scene I just described, and I felt outnumbered, outsmarted, and out of hope. Sometimes the Lord of Hosts comes to rescue in a dramatic way. Sometimes His angels are seen and other times they are unseen. And sometimes it feels like He decided not to show up. In these moments of seemingly temporary setbacks, I hope you will listen for the sounds coming from the mountains: the sounds of the Lord of Hosts mustering His great army. He has already defeated all of our enemies. We might have to wait for the final victory, but we can be certain it is coming with Jesus as the commander. —DB

Reflect and Respond

What battles are you facing in which you need victory? What hope do you have in an eventual rescue?

Your favorite scripture in 2 Nephi 23

2 NEPHI 24:3

And it shall come to pass in that day that
the Lord shall give thee rest.

Usually when I think of the word *rest*, I think of taking a nap. But recently I was reading Matthew 11:28, and that scripture caused me to reconsider. "Come unto me, all ye that labour and are heavy laden, and I will give you rest." What type of rest is He talking about?

It got me thinking about a cut crystal vase that was given to me from my grandmother. It is beautiful. It is one of my most prized possessions. I love to put flowers in it and place it right next to my bed.

I am careful with the vase because it is precious to me. I don't want it to get broken.

One afternoon when I was carrying the vase into my bedroom the word *rest* took on a whole new meaning for me. The vase was full of beautiful pink peonies. I wanted to show them off, and I hesitated next to a large shelf in my family room. They would be beautiful there; everyone would notice them when they came in the room. But I didn't trust the security of the shelf, at least not enough to rest the cut crystal vase there. That was when it hit me: we can't rest on something we don't trust.

Maybe that is the lesson of this verse. As we learn to trust the Lord, He will give us rest from fear, from sorrow, and from bondage.

We can rest in Him. —EBF

Reflect and Respond
How do you find rest in the Lord?

Your favorite
scripture in
2 Nephi 24

2 NEPHI 25:29

And now behold, I say unto you that
the right way is to believe in Christ.

One of Nephi's greatest passions is to teach about the importance of believing in Christ, "For we labor diligently to write, to persuade our children, and also our brethren, to believe in Christ, and to be reconciled to God" (2 Nephi 25:23). In fact, he is so invested in this passion that he devotes one whole chapter to the teaching of it. Within this chapter the phrase "believe in Christ" is mentioned six different times.

I love the list Nephi gives us for strengthening belief; it is in a verse that is beloved by many of us: "And we talk of Christ, we rejoice in Christ, we preach of Christ, we prophesy of Christ, and we write according to our prophecies, that our children may know to what source they may look for a remission of their sins" (2 Nephi 25:26). In our day, those descriptions might sound like this: we talk of Christ, rejoice in Christ, teach of Christ, testify of Christ, and write according to our testimonies, so that our children might know how to come unto Christ. Think about the counsel to have more Christ-centered teaching in the home. How many of your discussions follow this counsel from Nephi? How could this counsel improve your home-centered lessons?

At the end of this chapter, Nephi repeats his plea two times so we won't miss it. We find it first in verse 28, "For the right way is to believe in Christ and deny him not," and again in verse 29, "And now behold, I say unto you that the right way is to believe in Christ, and deny him not." —EBF

Reflect and Respond

Name one way you can talk of Christ, rejoice in Christ, teach or testify or write of Jesus Christ in your home-centered lesson this week.

Your favorite
scripture in
2 Nephi 25

2 NEPHI 26:33

For he doeth that which is good among the children of men; and he doeth nothing save it be plain unto the children of men; **and he inviteth them all to come unto him** and partake of his goodness.

During Jesus's earthly ministry, He was often criticized by religious leaders for the kind of people He chose to eat with. He would sit with outsiders, foreigners, sinners, and people with questionable reputations, and He would treat them like they were lifelong friends. In His day, the table where you ate was a table of fellowship. Eating with people was a social sign that you accepted those people just as they were. I imagine there were people back then—perhaps as many as we have today—who felt unwelcomed and uninvited. There are people who feel less than, and overlooked, and unloved.

There are a lot of things that are uncertain in this world, but I know of at least two things that will never change. First, you and I are always welcomed, invited, and loved by Jesus. We will always have a place at His table—no matter who we are, where we come from, or what we have done. The second thing I know for sure about Him is that all He does is for the good of the world. His heart and mind are set on it. And when I say the world, I mean everybody who is in it. Not just the lump sum of the population, but each and every person is specifically invited to come and sit with Him and partake of His goodness. When Jesus gets to the table, He looks around to see who is missing. —DB

Reflect and Respond

Is there someone you can invite or welcome to your table of fellowship today?

Your favorite scripture in 2 Nephi 26

_____

_____

2 NEPHI 27:23

**For behold, I am God;
and I am a God of miracles.**

The very fact that you are reading these words is evidence that God is a God of miracles. The words come from the Book of Mormon—a record that was kept and preserved for over a thousand years by ancient inhabitants of the Americas, buried in the ground, and then dug up 1400 years later and translated over the period of about two months by an uneducated farm boy. Later in 2 Nephi 27, the coming forth of the Book of Mormon and the accompanying Restoration of the gospel are referred to as a "marvelous work and a wonder." If we were to sit down and write the list of miracles that brought about the Restoration, it would be miles long. It was an unexpected and amazing task that God is still performing.

The same God who brought about the Restoration is the God we still worship. He is a God who performed great miracles in the past and is still performing them today. They are written in the hearts and journals of people all over the world. He can still do anything, anytime, anywhere. The coming forth of the Restoration and Book of Mormon is miraculous, but the greater miracles He is performing are in the hearts of men and women—His actual work and glory. The transformation of the human soul is the greatest work and the greatest wonder of all. —DB

Reflect and Respond
When have you experienced God as a God of miracles today?

Your favorite scripture in 2 Nephi 27

2 NEPHI 28:24

Therefore, wo be unto him that is at ease in Zion!

I once heard a commander talk about this verse and compare it to his time in the army. He talked about two phrases that are commonly used in the military: "stand at attention" and "at ease." If you know anything about the army, or if you have ever watched a movie about the military, you might recognize what this looks like. People are asked to "stand at attention" when a command is being given. It connotes engaging, focusing, and preparing to receive instruction. Usually when a group is called to "stand at attention," they are in straight lines, shoulders back, eyes focused on the commander, and hands down at their sides. Their attention is fixed on the person who is speaking. "At ease" is a phrase used after instruction has been given. It is a relaxing, a time of letting down your guard.

Chapter 28 of 2 Nephi is all about the last days. It warns us to beware of false churches, of foolish doctrines, of the apostasy that will abound, and of the devil raging. There is trouble on every side.

It is not a time to be at ease. This war on belief will require us to be ready, attentive, and prepared. It will require us to stand. —EBF

Reflect and Respond

Do a scripture study on the word stand *and list the counsel you find. How could those scriptures prepare your family for our day?*

Your favorite scripture in 2 Nephi 28

2 NEPHI 29:5

O ye Gentiles, have ye remembered the Jews, mine ancient covenant people? . . . **for I the Lord have not forgotten my people**.

Do you know someone who you trust will always remember to do what they said they would do? I am not one of those people. I am always forgetting to reply to emails, texts, and calls, to return things I borrowed, and to follow through on promises that I made earlier in the day. It is not that I don't care—I just forget. My grandma, on the other hand, is the exact opposite. If she says she will bring something, send something, or say something, you could bet your life on the fact that she will follow through with it. Her memory and dedication to remembering are as refreshing as my forgetfulness is frustrating. I feel confident in what she says she will do. And that brings my soul rest.

This is the character of the Lord. Throughout scripture, He has made covenants and promises about His chosen children. He has sworn that He will not leave them or forget them. As we read the history, we find long stretches when it seems like the Lord has more of my personality—that He has forgotten. But if we keep reading and waiting and watching, we see that He does intend to and always does fulfill all of His promises—especially when they have to do with the well-being of His children.

In the introduction to the Book of Mormon, we learn that the coming forth of that book is in and of itself a manifestation and evidence of God continually reaching out to His children—children He has not forgotten. —DB

Reflect and Respond

How have you seen that the Lord has not forgotten you?

Your favorite scripture in 2 Nephi 29

2 NEPHI 30:18

And Satan shall have power over the hearts of the
children of men **no more, for a long time**.

Can you imagine a period when Satan has no power for a long time? I long for that day.

Before that happens, the Lord tells us, "the time speedily cometh that the Lord God shall cause a great division among the people" (2 Nephi 30:10). It is a division that has to happen before Satan is bound. It will be a time of choosing, of standing with the Lord or against Him. A time of drawing a line in the sand and holding our ground . . . not against people, but against Satan.

As the final scenes begin to take place, we must set our feet in the ground and stand firm, but we must also love as many people over to the Lord's side of the line as we can. We must gather. We must provide a safe haven. We must have charity. It is how we fight against the side of wickedness until Satan is bound.

When the Lord comes, He will come with righteousness and faithfulness. The scriptures tell us about the wolf and the lamb, the leopard and the kid, and the calf and the young lion . . . and when I read about that time, there is no division, there is only love.

That's what it will feel like when Satan is bound.

Love. —EBF

Reflect and Respond

How can love help fight against division? What would the outcome be?

Your favorite
scripture in
2 Nephi 30

2 NEPHI 31:19

Ye have not come thus far save it were by the word of
Christ with unshaken faith in him, **relying wholly upon
the merits of him who is mighty to save**.

I did not call my parents to thank them for everything they did for me growing up until I had a baby of my own. I had no idea! I don't remember any of it—the diapers, the all-nighters, the feeding, the swings, the car seats, and all the rest of the things. Once I became a parent, I started to realize how much my parents sacrificed, loved, and watched over me. Newborn babies and little children are completely helpless on their own. Everything has to be done for them. Without someone to look out for their needs, they would never make it. Babies are completely reliant on someone else.

The same is true for us—especially and perhaps most importantly with our salvation. Concerning salvation, we are like babies—completely helpless on our own. In Nephi's words, we rely "wholly" or exclusively and fully upon the "merits" or works of Him— Jesus Christ—for our salvation. He is mighty and uses His might, mind, and strength to bring about our rescue and redemption.

No one is able to step in and take His place. Nephi said later, "There is none other way nor name given under heaven whereby man can be saved" (2 Nephi 31:21). Jesus is not only willing but also the only one capable of this saving mission. No one else can save us—not even ourselves. We can do good works to show love, but our merits cannot and will not be enough. We must rely wholly upon Him. —DB

Reflect and Respond

What are some ways you rely upon Him?

Your favorite
scripture in
2 Nephi 31

2 NEPHI 32:5

**. . . receive the Holy Ghost, it will show unto
you all things what ye should do.**

What is the best thing you ever brought to show-and-tell? One time I brought a little baby lamb. I was the hero of show-and-tell that day. Everyone wanted to pet it, and feed it a bottle, and ask all the questions. That particular show-and-tell led to a memorable experience that none of us would quickly forget.

Every time I read 2 Nephi 32, it reminds me of show-and-tell. Here is why:

"Wherefore, I said unto you, feast upon the words of Christ; for behold, the words of Christ will *tell* you all things what ye should do" (2 Nephi 32:3; emphasis added).

"For behold, again I say unto you that if ye will enter in by the way, and receive the Holy Ghost, it will *show* unto you all things what ye should do" (2 Nephi 32:5; emphasis added).

The scriptures will tell us what to do; the Holy Ghost will show us what we should do. It's God's own version of show-and-tell. The two combined together lead us to experiences that we won't forget. —EBF

Reflect and Respond

*Can you think of a time when the scriptures told you what to do
and the Holy Ghost showed you what to do? What was the outcome?*

Your favorite
scripture in
2 Nephi 32

2 NEPHI 33:6

I glory in plainness; I glory in truth; **I glory in my Jesus**,
for he hath redeemed my soul from hell.

I am so thrilled to have this little sneak peek into Nephi's heart at the end of His writings. From it, we get a sense of what made his heart soar: plainness, truth, and especially Jesus. I have always loved how Nephi does not just say Jesus, but *my Jesus*.

Think about the people in your life to whom you would attach that descriptive possessive word when describing them. Are you like me and you use it for a spouse? A child? A dear friend? Whenever I introduce someone who is close to me to others, I will use that word. *My* Jack. *My* Jenny. If you were to hear me use it and not know who those people were, you would probably assume that they were people I was endeared to. The word shows a closeness and tenderness when talking about someone.

This is why I love that Nephi uses that same word to talk about Jesus. *My Jesus.* It seems to say to me that there is a closeness and tenderness between them, something much more than a casual acquaintance. This was Someone who would redeem and rescue Nephi's soul. Someone who would snatch him out of the grasp of the adversary at a great cost. Someone who would be both willing and able to walk that road for Nephi. It seems like it is through this realization of what Jesus has done and will do that they become most acquainted—at least it is why Nephi tells us he glories so much in Him. His praise for Him is a response to the love that Jesus showed him first. —DB

Reflect and Respond

What are those things about Jesus that you glory in? What endears Him to you?

Your favorite
scripture in
2 Nephi 33

JACOB 1:17

. . . having first obtained mine errand from the Lord.

I have a neighbor who often needs me to run errands for her. Sometimes I pick up prescriptions from the pharmacy. I have dropped off a forgotten lunch to her son at school. My friend is blind, so she can't drive, and I am one of the people on her errand list. The best part of running the errands is the connection it has built between us. This would be true for all of the people on her list. We have each become her closest friends. We serve her by running her errands, but she serves us right back by listening, and encouraging, and cheerleading behind the scenes of everything we do. I can't help but wonder if the Lord has an errand list—a group of people He knows will respond if He reaches out to them with a need. It reminds me of a man named Joseph Millett.

Joseph Millett, with his large family, was suffering through very, very difficult times. He wrote in his journal: "One of my children came in and said that Brother Newton Hall's folks was out of bread, had none that day. I divided our flour in a sack to send up to Brother Hall. Just then Brother Hall came. Says I, 'Brother Hall, are you out of flour?' 'Brother Millett, we have none.' 'Well, Brother Hall, there is some in that sack. I have divided and was going to send it to you. Your children told mine that you was out.' Brother Hall began to cry. He said he had tried others, but could not get any. He went to the cedars and prayed to the Lord, and the Lord told him to go to Joseph Millett. 'Well Brother Hall, you needn't bring this back. If the Lord sent you for it you don't owe me for it.'" That night Joseph Millett recorded a remarkable sentence in his journal: "You can't tell me how good it made me feel to know that the Lord knew there was such a person as Joseph Millett" (Diary of Joseph Millett, holograph, Church History Library). —EBF

Reflect and Respond

Ask to be on the Lord's errand today, and then watch for opportunities.

Your favorite scripture in
Jacob 1

JACOB 2:8

And it supposeth me that they have come up hither to hear the pleasing word of God, yea, the **word which healeth the wounded soul**.

There is so much hurt in this world. It takes only a few minutes of watching the news or catching up with someone's life to realize how much sadness and pain are hidden away in people's hearts. There are tragedies, broken promises, trials, disease, and heartache of every kind. Just as a battle causes physical wounds, the battle of life can leave us with wounds in our soul—wounds that need as much attention and care (if not more) as the hurt that is physically visible with people.

The prophet Jacob acted as a doctor of the soul and taught us that one of the ways that leads to healing is to hear the pleasing word of God. Other professional help is available and needed when we have been hurt or betrayed in some ways, but the promises and hope that God gives us through scripture and whispers of the Spirit can please, calm, and help with the healing.

I have known people who have held on to promises found in the pages of scripture and in the words of blessings that have given them strength. I have known others who have felt their broken hearts being put back together as they read and heard of the extravagant love of God as it was preached from pulpits and shared in late-afternoon text messages from friends. God is so good and so brilliant in His glory that even His words have the power to enter our hearts and begin to heal them. —DB

Reflect and Respond

Which promises of God have given you strength? Do you know someone who needs healing that you could read or send His words to?

Your favorite scripture in Jacob 2

JACOB 3:2

Feast upon his love; for ye may, if your minds are firm, forever.

Recently I have been studying what it means to live vertically as opposed to living horizontally.

Living horizontally is to live life looking sideways. We take our suggestions and our counsel from those who we associate with. The world becomes our standard. Living horizontally can be painful. Ask anyone who has ever done a belly flop: entering the water horizontally hurts.

Living vertically is to live life looking up. The first two verses of Jacob 3 define what it might look like to live vertically:

1. Look unto God with firmness of mind
2. Pray unto him with exceeding faith
3. Lift up your heads
4. Receive the pleasing word of God
5. Feast upon His love

These five things will help our minds become firm—forever. It is an interesting list, and more simple than we might first assume. Look to God, pray, lift up your head, receive His word, and immerse yourself in His love. It is an excellent formula for living vertically. —EBF

Reflect and Respond

Which of the items on the list are you good at? Which need more work? Choose one to work on this week.

Your favorite scripture in Jacob 3

JACOB 4:7

Nevertheless, the Lord God showeth us our weakness **that we may know that it is by his grace**, and his great condescensions unto the children of men, that we have power to do these things.

I think most people like getting compliments. Don't you? Do you like to hear about how good you are at something? Or what a benefit you are to an organization? Or that your talents and gifts are appreciated and desperately needed? Hearing this type of talk not only warms my heart but gives me confidence to face new challenges and tackle old problems. Having our strengths validated is so valuable.

So is learning about our weaknesses—at least, that is what the Lord thinks. Most of us don't want to learn about our weaknesses, especially if someone else shows us what they are. It hurts our pride, our ego, and our confidence when someone points out where we are falling short. So why does the Lord do it? According to Jacob, He does it to show us His grace. If we thought we were doing everything with our own strength and wisdom, we wouldn't even need or want a saving God. But when we learn that we simply cannot do it on our own, our hearts start to reach up and out for help—and He reaches our reaching. When we know we are incapable, we can see more clearly His infinite wisdom and love working on our behalf—and we feel watched over and loved. Only when we cry for help do we begin to sense how much help He has been giving all along. —DB

Reflect and Respond

What are some of the tasks and journeys you are on right now that you have realized you cannot do on your own?

Your favorite scripture in Jacob 4

JACOB 5:49

. . . for I have done all.

My favorite way to read Jacob 5 is to look for verses that teach me about the character of Christ, the master of the vineyard.

The first lesson can be found in a word that is repeated twenty times in this chapter, a word that is the main concern for the master of the vineyard. He repeats the word *preserve* over and over again, " . . . that I may preserve it unto mine own self" (Jacob 5:20). This is a master intent on saving.

The second lesson is the master's worry over every single tree: "It grieveth me that I should lose this tree" (Jacob 5:7). He doesn't say "these trees," He says "this tree"—this is a master concerned about the one.

The third lesson is that the master of the vineyard doesn't give up. "For behold, said he, this long time have I nourished it" (Jacob 5:20). He tells us over and over again how He has nourished His trees this long time.

The fourth lesson has to do with what the master of the vineyard is willing to do to save the trees. It is a tender moment when He weeps and asks, "What could I have done more for my vineyard?" (Jacob 5:41). Then He reminds us, "I have done all" (Jacob 5:49). This is a master who is willing to give all for His vineyard.

The last lesson is found toward the end of the chapter in verses 60–63. Here we see another repetition; this time the repeated word is *again*. We learn that the master gives second chances, and third chances, and as many chances as it might take to save the tree.

Every time I read the allegory of the olive tree I am reminded how much I love the master of the vineyard. —EBF

Reflect and Respond

Consider the characteristics of Christ that we learn from this chapter. What is the master doing in your vineyard?

Your favorite scripture in Jacob 5

JACOB 6:12

O be wise; what can I say more?

Sometimes at weddings, or baby showers, or graduation dinners, there is a tradition of all the guests giving one bit of advice to the person who is entering a new phase of life. It is always tough to narrow down your experiences to one simple, memorable, and meaningful life lesson. When I read this line of scripture from the prophet Jacob, I imagine him standing up in one of these life milestone events and giving this piece of advice: *Be wise.*

Wisdom is sometimes defined as the proper application of knowledge—to make decisions that are in harmony with the truth that you know. In this particular chapter, Jacob explained the redemption and rescue that come to a person who chooses to receive Jesus Christ. Only in and through His name can a person avoid the consequences of sin and death. That is the truth. And then he gives us this advice—be wise. Choose Jesus. What else can he say that would have more impact and more long-lasting joy than that simple decision to choose Him, based on that beautiful truth that it is only in and through Him that we can be saved? —DB

Reflect and Respond
What impact has choosing Jesus had in your life? Why would you advise other people to choose Him?

Your favorite scripture in Jacob 6

JACOB 7:5

I had heard the voice of the Lord speaking unto me in very word, from time to time; **wherefore, I could not be shaken**.

A careful reading of this chapter helps us remember how determined Sherem is to shake the faith of Jacob. What is noteworthy is why Jacob tells us he can't be shaken. He talks about:

- having faith in Christ
- the power of revelation
- the ministering of angels
- the voice of the Lord speaking from time to time

One morning before class started, I asked my seminary kids to write a tender mercy in their journals: a time when they had seen God's hand working in their lives, maybe an answer to a prayer. Once they were done, I walked up to one of the students and asked a question, "What if I told you that experience didn't really happen?"

His response was immediate: "I would tell you that you were wrong."

"What if I told you it happened, but it didn't come from God?"

"You would be wrong." Again, the response was immediate.

"Is there anything I could say that would talk you out of believing this was a tender mercy sent from the Lord?"

"Nothing." His response was solid.

"Hold on to that journal entry for the rest of your life," I told him. "Those personal experiences with the Lord are what will keep you from being shaken."

It was true for Jacob. It is just as true for each one of us. —EBF

Reflect and Respond

Consider the four things that kept Jacob's faith from being shaken. Which of those have strengthened your faith?

Your favorite scripture in Jacob 7

ENOS 1:9

I began to feel a desire for the welfare of my brethren, the Nephites; wherefore, **I did pour out my whole soul** unto God for them.

The story of Enos going into the forest and wrestling before God in an emotional and mighty spiritual struggle is one of the greatest chapters on prayer in scripture. There have been times in my life when I have been able to relate so deeply to him. In his own words, Enos described a "wrestle which I had before God" (Enos 1:2). To me, it has always been important that Enos was not wrestling *with* God but rather *before* God. They were not enemies or at odds with each other. Enos was struggling with something in his life, and he was working through it in the presence of God—in the shadow of His strength and grace. There have been times in my life when I have not needed someone to solve my problem for me, but rather I just needed them near. Their presence was gift enough.

At this time in his life, Enos was worried about his own salvation, the salvation of his friends and family, and even the salvation of his enemies. I love the words he uses to describe his prayers on behalf of his brothers: "I did pour out my whole soul unto God." The imagery of pouring out everything in your heart—to empty it all before the Lord—is moving and powerful. And it is precisely what the Lord wants: our whole soul. All of our questions, our hopes, our doubts, our ambitions, our fears—everything. He wants us to come before him with vulnerability and authenticity. To be honest and to be open. To pour out. —DB

Reflect and Respond

What do you have in your soul to pour out before the Lord?

Your favorite scripture in Enos 1

JAROM 1:3

Behold, it is expedient that **much should be done** among this people.

It wasn't the first time she had been diagnosed with cancer. She had battled it her entire life. But the thought of another surgery, of chemo and radiation, of another recovery was almost more than she could handle. There were other things in her life she would rather focus on: things around the house, things with her children, things with her husband's work. Now, all those things would have to wait.

An institute class she attended heard about the surgery, about the cancer, about the long recovery ahead, and asked how they could help. Some signed up to plant petunias; others volunteered to weed the garden. Someone knew how to tile the backsplash. Another mended the deck. Carpet was laid, and paint was applied, and new doorknobs were installed. And it all happened in two weeks, before the surgery even took place, so that when she returned home she could focus on recovering because all the other things were taken care of.

It was expedient that much should be done . . . and it was. All the little things.

It doesn't matter where we live, if we open our eyes and our hearts we will discover the needs of the people who live around us. The Lord can open our eyes; He can help us find those who are struggling. He can help us work miracles and take care of all the little things.

He knows there is much to be done.

He will use us if we ask. —EBF

Reflect and Respond

Open your eyes and your heart . . . where is there much to be done?
What could you do?

Your favorite scripture in Jarom 1

OMNI 1:26

And now, my beloved brethren, I would that ye should come unto Christ, who is the Holy One of Israel, and partake of his salvation, and the power of his redemption. Yea, come unto him, and **offer your whole souls as an offering unto him**.

The legendary football coach Vince Lombardi once said, "I firmly believe that any man's finest hour, the greatest fulfillment of all that he holds dear, is that moment when he has worked his heart out in a good cause and lies exhausted on the field of battle—victorious."

I spent many days as a full-time missionary thinking of this advice, and it would motivate me to keep pushing through a particularly tough day or experience. When doors were not opened, when people did not show up, and when our prayers and hopes did not seem to be answered, I often felt like quitting. But I would push through the disappointments and discouragements until the sun had gone down and the day was over. On most nights, but particularly on those discouraging ones, I would get to my bedside, kneel down, and offer up a prayer that went like this: "Heavenly Father—I don't have much to show, but I sure tried to give everything I had today." And then I would slip into my covers, exhausted and worn out, and fall asleep the happiest person in the world.

This was the pattern set by Jesus, who came into the world and, because of His love for the Father, gave all. He worked his heart out in a good cause—the best cause—and came away victorious. He gave His whole soul as an offering and simply hopes for the same in return. All for all. —DB

Reflect and Respond

What will be your offering to God today? What will be your good cause?

Your favorite scripture in Omni 1

WORDS OF MORMON 1:7

He worketh in me
to do according to his will.

Michelangelo had a talent for taking a block of marble and chiseling away the unnecessary while keeping the form until he had finally exposed the beauty within. He once said, "I saw the angel in the marble and carved until I set him free."

Imagine having that kind of talent—the ability to look at a rough-hewn block of marble and chip away at it until its true beauty is discovered.

Perhaps this is a good analogy for how the Lord works in our lives. He sees what we can become, He knows our gifts and our possibilities, and He knows just what it will take to help us reach our potential. When He looks us over, He knows what needs to go and also what parts to keep. We are the work of His hand, His finest creation, a masterpiece.

I love how Mormon reminds us that the Lord works in us, because sometimes we forget. We forget He is the master of creation. The author and finisher of our stories. The one who knows all things, including all the things He has in mind for us to do and to become.

On those days when we forget, maybe we can call to memory the words of Paul and find peace, "being confident of this very thing, that he which hath begun a good work in you will perform it" (Philippians 1:6). —EBF

Reflect and Respond
How have you felt Him working in you? What have you accomplished because of Him?

Your favorite scripture in Words of Mormon 1

_____

_____

MOSIAH 1:6

**We can know of their surety because
we have them before our eyes.**

When my children were little, I had a hard time setting aside time for personal scripture study. When the night came I was too tired, and the mornings always began with someone crying for my attention. Daytime was a circus, but I could sometimes squeeze in my reading during naptime along with everything else that had to be done in those few free minutes.

Then one day I found a solution. I started leaving my scriptures open and carrying them from room to room, wherever I was. If I was making peanut butter and jelly sandwiches, I would lay them on the kitchen counter, read one verse, and ponder it while everyone ate lunch. If I was doing laundry, I would put them next to my pile, and again, I would read one verse and ponder as I sorted. Truthfully, I still only got in several verses a day, but the difference was that I was taking time to ponder them. The beauty of having my scriptures open everywhere I went was that I could immediately pick up where I had left off, and the open book became an invitation to reengage.

I love the scriptures. I teach them for a profession. Some people have introduced me as a scriptorian. You might be interested to know that I didn't go to school in theology, I don't have any formal instruction, I am not a professor of religion. My knowledge of the scriptures came because they were continually before my eyes. The Spirit tutored me alongside the laundry and the dishes and the changing of diapers. He will do the same for you. —EBF

Reflect and Respond

Try leaving your scriptures open for a few days and see if it makes a difference in your study habits. What do you notice?

Your favorite
scripture in
Mosiah 1

MOSIAH 2:24

He doth require that ye should do as he hath commanded you;
for which if ye do, **he doth immediately bless you**.

I don't like to be "outgifted." I never want someone else to give me a gift that is better, more thoughtful, or more expensive than the gift I give to them. If it happens, I feel indebted to them—like I owe them something more. I am admitting this, but also admitting that I realize it is not a positive trait to have. This is especially true if we apply it to our relationship with God.

King Benjamin taught us that we are all indebted to God. He created us, gave us life, and lends us breath every moment of all our days. For that, we can never repay Him. All He asks is that we follow Him and keep His commandments. And when we do, He "immediately" blesses us for doing it. Interestingly, His commandments are all given to us for our benefit—so even the commandments themselves are blessings. As we try to show love for what He has done for us (by keeping those commandments), He immediately shows more love in return. Even if we tried to "pay Him back," we would always stay unprofitable and in His debt. It is impossible to match His goodness. He has always and will always outgift us. All He hopes for in return is our love and our loyalty. And a grateful heart. —DB

Reflect and Respond

What immediate blessings have you seen from the Lord as you have kept His commandments?

Your favorite scripture in Mosiah 2

MOSIAH 3:3

**For behold, I am come to declare unto
you the glad tidings of great joy.**

Did you wonder, for just a second, if you were reading the Christmas story in Luke 2? It is repeated again here in Mosiah. The message comes from an angel, but instead of appearing to shepherds in a field, this angel appears to King Benjamin. He has come to announce a time, not far distant, when the Lord will come down from heaven, will be born on earth, and will work mighty miracles—healing the sick, raising the dead, giving sight to the blind, and healing the lame and the deaf.

The declaration of glad tidings of great joy in Mosiah matches the one in Luke 2, that Jesus will come, that He will meet us where we are, that He will enter into our stories and help us find the way back home.

It is what Jesus does best. Think of your favorite New Testament story about Jesus. The woman at the well, Peter walking on water, the man at the pool of Bethesda, the man blind from birth, the man at the Gadarenes. Picture it in your mind. Consider the location, what the person looked like, the people who were there. Now, think about this—where was Jesus? At the well. In the water. On the steps of the pool. Kneeling in the dirt. Walking through the tombs. He met all of those individuals where they were, as they were, but He didn't intend to leave them there. Through grace, He offered to take them to places they could never arrive at on their own.

These are the glad tidings of great joy. —EBF

Reflect and Respond

Can you think of a time when the Lord entered into your story?
What happened?

Your favorite
scripture in
Mosiah 3

MOSIAH 4:19

For behold, **are we not all beggars**? Do we not all depend upon the same
Being, even God, for all the substance which we have, for both food and raiment,
and for gold, and for silver, and for all the riches which we have of every kind?

My cousin, who passed away too early in life, always had a soft spot for the unfortunate. Each year on his birthday, to honor the way he lived, members of our extended family plan and carry out some sort of service project for those who are in need. He had such a gift to see them as he would anyone else. When others turned their faces away, he would look into people's eyes. Even if he had nothing to give, he always treated them like equals. Like brothers and sisters in the great family of God.

I admit, when I see someone holding a sign near the on-ramp at the freeway, it is difficult for me to know how to help. I struggle wondering if they really are in need, or how they would use any money I decided to give them. My heart breaks at the same time my mind plays the skeptic. Sometimes I want there to be one answer—a formula I can apply to every situation. But that won't ever happen, because they are people, not equations. The logistics will always be different, but one thing will be constant—love. I remember King Benjamin's question: "Are we not all beggars?" And then I remember the times I have knelt on my closet floor or by my bedside pleading with God for help. Begging. I may as well have been holding a sign. —DB

Reflect and Respond

*How does remembering our own pleadings to God change the way
we see and treat others?*

Your favorite
scripture in
Mosiah 4

MOSIAH 5:12

I would that ye should **remember to retain the name** written always in your hearts.

When my children were born, we wanted their names to have great meaning. As we thought about the names they would be known by, we came up with two guidelines—one name would be that of someone we admired, the other would come from scripture. Each of my children has both a Bible name and the name of a close family member or friend. Each name is a reminder of who they can become.

For many years a sign hung in our home that would remind my children about their names: "Be true to who you are and the family name you bear" (Gordon B. Hinckley). We talked often about the power that is in a name.

In Mosiah, King Benjamin teaches a similar principle. He invited each one of us to take upon us the name of Christ, but he didn't just want us to take it, He wanted us to remember to hold onto the name so that we would hear and know the voice by which we would be called and the name by which He would call us. This name, too, becomes a reminder of who we can become.

Every Sunday we have the opportunity to take His name. Instead of a sign hanging on the wall of our homes to remind us, we participate in an ordinance in which we promise to take His name, remember Him, and keep His commandments. Mosiah tells us this pattern of taking His name, retaining or remembering it, and hearing His voice will lead us to know the Lord.

That is the blessing that comes from writing His name in our hearts. —EBF

Reflect and Respond

Consider reading Mosiah 5 as you prepare to take the sacrament this week as a reminder of what it means to take His name.

Your favorite scripture in Mosiah 5

MOSIAH 6:7

And king Mosiah did cause his people that they should till the earth. **And he also, himself, did till the earth**, that thereby he might not become burdensome to his people, that he might do according to that which his father had done in all things.

My sons have a favorite baseball team. It happens to be my favorite team as well. And as you might guess, it is my dad's favorite team, and my grandfather's favorite team also. It is a tradition that is passed down in our family. It is much like the tradition that passed down through the family of kings in this part of the Book of Mormon.

Mosiah, the new king of the Nephites, was known for getting his hands dirty out in the fields. He learned that from his own father, King Benjamin. It would be easy for a king to spend his days in the shade on a cushion, but Mosiah learned from his dad what it meant to be a leader—what it meant to serve, to share the burdens of the people, to till side by side in the fields as equals. I wonder if King Benjamin learned that same lesson from *his* father—a lesson Jesus would one day teach when he said that the "greatest among you shall be your servant" (Matthew 23:11).

My wife's grandfather raised his children in Hawaii. During their time there, he was called as a leader and was quickly given the nickname "the taro patch bishop." Most of the bishops organized the work of picking the taro plants and left the digging to the locals. But not this one. He started a tradition in his family of what it meant to be a servant leader, just like Mosiah. A tradition that still carries on today. —DB

Reflect and Respond

In what ways have you seen service as the greatest form of leadership?

Your favorite scripture in Mosiah 6

MOSIAH 7:12

I will endeavor to **speak with boldness**.

Several years ago, I reached out to a woman who leads a Christian conference in Texas. She is a woman I greatly admire, and I expressed my gratitude for her work and asked for some advice. She responded to my email by saying that she had never spoken to "anyone who is Mormon" before and wondered if I had time for a one-hour phone call.

I was scared to death. I instantly regretted sending the email. How would I know what to say? What if I didn't have all the answers? Why did the Lord lead me into this situation when there were obviously people more qualified than I was?

I spent the next three days praying that the Spirit would help me know how to respond to each of the questions. On that Thursday, before the phone call began, I said a prayer and asked for an increase of the Holy Ghost so I would know what to do and say and so that I would have courage. I wanted to speak with boldness.

My friend asked two questions. The first was, "What is different about our two religions?" The second was, "What is similar?" The conversation was intense, but also filled with love and acceptance. Just before the phone call ended, she said to me, "I like you, and our door will always be open for you." I felt a sweet sense of confirmation and gratitude that the Spirit had helped me be bold. After that conversation, I thought to myself, *I might be the only Latter-day Saint she ever meets.* I hope I was a good one. —EBF

Reflect and Respond

Think of a time in your life when you have endeavored to speak with boldness. What did you learn?

Your favorite scripture in Mosiah 7

MOSIAH 8:19

When Ammon had made an end of speaking these words the king rejoiced exceedingly, and gave thanks to God, saying: **Doubtless a great mystery is contained within these plates**.

When I was growing up, on Christmas mornings, there were often small presents that had been wrapped up and placed gently on the Christmas tree branches or tucked deep underneath and behind all the other gifts. These were always opened last. We never knew what they were, but we all always knew that they were going to be the best ones—especially if my mom got the camera out to take our picture as we opened them. It was a mystery, but we knew it was going to be a thrilling one.

When Ammon discovered the people of Limhi, he was presented with a collection of records that had been found before he got there. They were in a different language and couldn't be read, but Ammon told the people that the king of his land had the gift of interpreting them. This is what caused the king and his people to rejoice and thank God. No one knew what was going to be on those plates, but they were certain it was going to be great—a great mystery!

This is always true about God. We have no idea what He has in store for us tomorrow. What we will experience next remains a mystery. But one thing is doubtless—it is going to be great. And that is because of who God is. We can anticipate it and expect it every time. —DB

Reflect and Respond

What experiences have you had with the Lord that led you to anticipate that He has great things in store for you?

Your favorite scripture in Mosiah 8

MOSIAH 9:18

And God did hear our cries and did answer our prayers; and we did go forth in his might.

We were in an airport when we got the phone call. The older grandchildren had just finished a trip with Grandma and Grandpa. I had come along to act as tour guide. My sister's youngest had fallen into the pool while she was focused on taking off his sister's life jacket. By the time they got to him and pulled him out, he was unresponsive. An ambulance had come. He was en route to the hospital. They didn't think he would live.

I remember gathering around as we received the news. I remember the tears in the eyes of his siblings. I remember standing in a family circle in the middle of the busy airport terminal to pray, and then we boarded the plane. It would be two hours before we received the news that he had been revived, that all was well. For two hours we trusted the might of the Lord in behalf of little Will.

Prayer is a remarkable thing. It amazes me that we can speak with the God of the universe wherever we are and ask for whatever we need. It might be in a bedroom, or a church, or on a busy street, or in an airport terminal. It doesn't matter where we cry out to Him, the promise is the same: He will hear and help. Prayer is a remarkable gift from a loving Father to His child in need. *Reach out to me whenever and wherever you need me,* He invites every one of us, *and I will be there.* —EBF

Reflect and Respond
Read the entry on "Prayer" in the Bible Dictionary and journal about what you learn. How will it affect your personal prayers?

Your favorite scripture in Mosiah 9

MOSIAH 10:13

...and all this because that Nephi was more faithful in keeping the commandments of the Lord—**therefore he was favored of the Lord**, for the Lord heard his prayers and answered them.

Sometimes as siblings we joke with each other about who the favorite child is in our family. We even keep a ranking system. When my brother moved with his kids (the grandkids!) to where my parents live, he moved up in the ranking. My parents always tell us that there is no ranking and that all of us are their favorites. The jury is still out on whether my parents have favorites or not, but I am thoroughly convinced and certain that our Heavenly Parents do not.

Throughout the Book of Mormon we read the phrase *favored of the Lord.* At first glance, it seems like this line teaches that God might have favorites. But to be favored is different than being a favorite. *Favorite* implies loving one more than others. But God loves all of His children. His privileges and promises are equally available to each and every one of them. In this verse, we get a part of the definition of "being favored." Nephi was favored because he was more faithful in keeping the commandments, and that allowed the Lord to hear his prayers and answer them. How many of our prayers does the Lord hear? How many of them does He answer? Having God involved in our lives is the definition of being favored. Inviting Him, speaking with Him, and enjoying the presence of His Spirit are choices that each of us can decide to make. —DB

Reflect and Respond
In what ways have you sensed God's favor or presence in your life?

Your favorite scripture in Mosiah 10

MOSIAH 11:27

. . . who is Abinadi . . . who is the Lord?

This is one of my favorite lines in the King Noah story. The story begins by telling us everything we need to know about King Noah. He did not walk in the ways of his father; he cared only about the desires of his own heart. He caused his people to commit sin and do all manner of wickedness. All the taxes of his people went to support his own wants, which were filled with laziness, idolatry, whoredoms, and iniquity. He had many elegant buildings and a spacious palace.

Then Abinadi came among them and taught the people about the Lord who would deliver them from trouble if they turned to Him. Instead of inspiring the people, Abinadi's words made them angry—so angry that they wanted to kill Abinadi. When King Noah heard about Abinadi, he asked two important questions: *Who is Abinadi?* and *Who is the Lord?* The intent behind those two questions was to ask the importance, the power, and the might of each. In King Noah's eyes he was more important, more powerful, and more mighty than either the prophet or the Lord.

It wouldn't take long before he would realize he was wrong.

Do we ever underestimate the power of the Lord and His prophet? Do we look to them for advice and direction? Do we heed their counsel in our lives?

If you were to consider those two questions in our time and put some thought into answering them, what would your response be? Who is the prophet? Who is the Lord? How have their words impacted your life? —EBF

Reflect and Respond

What is the most recent counsel you have followed from the Lord and His prophet? How has it blessed your life?

Your favorite scripture in Mosiah 11

MOSIAH 12:8

And it shall come to pass that **except they repent I will utterly destroy them** from off the face of the earth.

Some verses of scripture are more difficult to swallow than others. This is one of those. I like to read about a God who loves, not a God who destroys. But rather than turn away from the verses when God says something that seems contrary to His nature and character, I like to explore them a little more. The fact that they are puzzling means there is something I don't know yet, something I need to study and exercise faith in until I do. The waiting and exploring usually lead to truths I didn't know before, and those truths are never disappointing.

The part I love most about this verse is the phrase *except they repent*. There are natural consequences to sin and rebellion. We believe in justice, and evil cannot be ignored. But there is a way out if we choose. We can turn from that course. We can change our paths. Jesus gives us another option, an exception—we can repent and turn back to Him.

Whatever life brings, or whatever choices we make, because of Jesus, there is always an "except." Reason and law and common sense might dictate a certain destiny for us, but His love allows another way. We can receive miracles, avoid certain types of pain, and receive second chances because of Him. —DB

Reflect and Respond

Are you possibly on a path that you want or need to turn from? What are some first steps you could take?

Your favorite scripture in Mosiah 12

MOSIAH 13:3

I have not delivered the message which the Lord sent me to deliver;
neither have I told you that which ye requested that I should tell.

One year I was asked to speak in our stake conference. Elder Bruce C. Hafen was to be our visiting General Authority. Because he is someone I admire greatly, I spent hours the week before the conference preparing my talk. I wanted it to be just right.

After the adult session of the conference on Saturday night, our stake president asked to visit with the people who would be speaking on Sunday. His direction was intimidating. Elder Hafen had asked him to tell us to throw away the messages we had prepared and begin again, with full reliance on what the Spirit wanted our messages to be. He took away our assigned topics. We were invited to go in any direction we felt impressed. It was the night before. Because I love and admire Elder Hafen so much, I did exactly what he asked. I threw away my talk and started over.

I felt prompted to speak on 2 Nephi 25:26. Elder Hafen followed by speaking on 2 Nephi 25:23, a verse that complemented the one I had chosen. After the meeting was over, he approached me and shook my hand. Then he asked, "How did you know what I would be speaking on? Your talk led right into mine." I didn't have any idea that was what he would be speaking on, but the Spirit did. In that moment, the power of the Spirit was impressed upon me in great detail. I don't know if anyone else was affected by my message that day, but I won't ever forget how it had been directed by the Spirit of the Lord. That one moment changed my life. It changed the way I prepare every talk I give. I learned to trust that the Spirit really will help you deliver the message the Lord wants you to deliver, and I try to rely completely on what the Spirit wants my message to be. —EBF

Reflect and Respond

Has there been a time when the Spirit has sent a message to your heart? What was that experience like?

Your favorite scripture in Mosiah 13

MOSIAH 14:3-5

He is despised and rejected of men; **a man of sorrows, and acquainted with grief**.... Surely he has borne our griefs, and carried our sorrows.... and with his stripes we are healed.

When the priests of the misguided King Noah brought the prophet Abinadi into their courts, they tried to overwhelm him with questions from a difficult passage in the writings of Isaiah. As part of his response, Abinadi quoted to them an entire mini sermon from Isaiah on the sacrifice of Jesus Christ.

These words that Isaiah first wrote and Abinadi then spoke to the priests are some of the most beautiful verses on the Savior's gift that can be found in ancient scripture. The prophecy of what Jesus would come to do is filled with descriptive words that turn my heart to Him with more tenderness and gratitude. In His life He was despised, rejected, stricken, wounded and filled with sorrow and grief so that in my life I could be healed, carried, and filled with peace.

Jesus's sacrifice was for all of mankind. Isaiah and Abinadi include themselves when they use the word *our* throughout the teaching. Consider reading through the verses again and exchanging the second-person words like *our* for first-person words like *my* to give the description a more personal application: "Surely He hath borne my griefs . . . my sorrows." —DB

Reflect and Respond

Which parts of this description of Jesus Christ's Atonement speak most personally to you?

Your favorite scripture in Mosiah 14

MOSIAH 15:18

. . . the founder of peace, yea, even the Lord . . .

I will never forget a particularly hard season of my life. Things were difficult. We were carrying a hard burden and we weren't sure how things would turn out. There was a lot of hurt and heartache and uncertainty. Perhaps you have had seasons like that?

On one particularly hard day, I was returning home from the grocery store. I was listening to a favorite song on repeat because the lyrics promised that everything would turn out all right, and one day I would find myself dancing through the storm. It was raining outside, and I pulled into my driveway wondering if this hard season would ever end. I can remember sitting in my car in my driveway, watching the windshield wipers go back and forth, eating a bag of Fritos, and just crying. Please say you have had days like that.

A couple of days later, I was studying the names of Christ in the Topical Guide and I stumbled across one I had never seen before: *Shiloh*. It's found in Genesis 49:10, and it means tranquility or peace. In the days following and for many weeks after I held onto that name. I whispered it in particularly hard moments, and every time I said it, I was reminded that peace isn't a feeling, it's a person. It's Jesus Christ. He is the founder of peace.

I don't know what your life looks like today. Hopefully it doesn't include rain and a bag of Fritos. But if it does, hold onto this: the peace you are seeking will come through Him. —EBF

Reflect and Respond

When has the Savior brought peace into your life?

Your favorite scripture in Mosiah 15

MOSIAH 16:6

And now if Christ had not come into the world, **speaking of things to come as though they had already come**, there could have been no redemption.

When Abinadi said these words, it was 150 years *before* the Savior was ever born to the earth. Yet he spoke them as if they were a past event. Can you imagine using that same speaking philosophy and style about other things? What if I spoke about tomorrow's basketball game victory as if it had already happened? They won! (When the tipoff is still 24 hours away.) As Abinadi continued his teaching, he said something similar about Christ's Resurrection: "If Christ had not risen from the dead, . . . there could have been no resurrection" (Mosiah 16:7). Again, both future events.

One of the things I love about the Book of Mormon is how many of the prophets and writers wrote and taught through a lens of hope. Lehi spoke of inheriting the promised land before they ever built a boat. Each of the prophets looked forward with anticipation as well as expectation. They lived *as if*. Because of who God is, there is a certainty about His promises that allows us to speak about them in present or past tense when they are still in the future.

No other person, team, or organization can give us that same level of hopeful confidence. We cannot make those same assumptions about anyone else. But with God, there are things that are certain. Things we can hope for. Things we can look forward to as if they had already happened. —DB

Reflect and Respond

What do you look forward to with hopeful anticipation? What certainties are in store for you because of our good God?

Your favorite scripture in Mosiah 16

MOSIAH 17:2

But there was one . . .

Have you ever wondered what kind of influence a testimony can have?

Abinadi spent day after day testifying of Jesus Christ to crowds, to the leaders of the kingdom, to the people in the streets. He would give his life for what he believed. Up to the very last moment, he was testifying of Jesus Christ. And then, just before Abinadi was taken to his death, we read that "there was one among them . . . a young man, and he believed" (Mosiah 16:2).

After all of those days preaching, after all of the persecution, after giving his life, Abinadi had converted only one who believed.

You might ask, was it worth it?

That one young man was Alma. He would take over where Abinadi left off, and his son would carry on after him, leaving an entire book of scripture containing his words and the details of his life and the legacy he left behind. All because of the testimony of one man.

In God's eyes, one is a powerful number. There is nothing He wouldn't do to save just one soul. Sister Elaine Dalton once said, "I truly believe that one virtuous young woman or young man, led by the Spirit, can change the world" ("A Return to Virtue," *Ensign*, November 2008). One.

You might think you are insignificant or unimportant. You might think your influence is small. You might wonder if you have anything to offer. You might just be one.

But one is all God needs. —EBF

Reflect and Respond

How does it make you feel to know the difference one person can make?

Your favorite scripture in Mosiah 17

MOSIAH 18:11

And now when the people had heard these words, **they clapped their hands for joy**, and exclaimed: This is the desire of our hearts.

I remember sitting in my living room on general conference weekend absolutely fixed to the TV while listening to a Saturday morning sermon from a leader whom I admire. When her talk was finished, I jumped to my feet and cheered. I really did. I clapped my hands and then threw them up into the air in victory. Her talk spoke to my soul, and it was a message I thought the entire world needed to hear.

When Alma explained to the people he was teaching what it meant to join the church of God and continue the covenant path through baptism, the people had a similar response. They clapped their hands in excitement and enthusiastically declared that it was the desire of their hearts to enter the covenant waters. It thrilled them to promise to mourn with those that mourn, to comfort the comfortless, and to stand as witnesses of the love of God throughout their whole lives. They couldn't wait to feel immersed in forgiveness, grace, and holiness, and to become citizens in His kingdom.

I have often thought that if the truths and promises of the gospel of Christ are taught correctly, they should lead people to excitement, anticipation, and clapping. God and His gospel are such good news, that news should move us to our feet—we should stand all amazed! —DB

Reflect and Respond

What is good news to you about a covenant relationship with God?

Your favorite scripture in Mosiah 18

MOSIAH 19:4

Gideon . . . he being a strong man . . .

There are some heroes in the Book of Mormon that we cannot pass by. Gideon is one of those. Every time he is mentioned, we see him standing for good. The first time we meet him, he is introduced as a strong man and an enemy to King Noah. Next, we find out he was King Limhi's captain, and that the king listened to and respected his counsel. He was responsible for coming up with the plan for getting the Nephites out of Lamanite bondage. They are all good stories, but Gideon's last story is my favorite. A man named Nehor began preaching in a manner that caused many people to leave the church. Then Gideon showed up. He was introduced as a man who believed in the church of God—a teacher. When Gideon approached, Nehor began to argue with him, hoping to lead more people away from the church. Here is the best line: "But the man withstood him, admonishing him with the words of God" (Alma 1:7).

When my son Josh was preparing to leave on his mission, he spent hours poring over the scriptures in order to find his mission scripture. The scripture he chose was about Gideon. Because he was a strong man. Because he was a captain to the king. Because he led people out of captivity. Because he withstood those who didn't believe and admonished them with the words of God. They were all descriptions of the missionary Josh wanted to be.

My boys are collectors of heroes. They will argue to no end about which superhero would beat which in combat. But movie heroes aren't the only heroes on their list. Gideon, Captain Moroni, and the stripling warriors are all men my boys have revered. There is something motivating about people who are strong, who stand up for what they believe, who are willing to admonish people with the word of God. —EBF

Reflect and Respond

The Book of Mormon is full of heroes. Who is one of yours and why?

Your favorite scripture in Mosiah 19

MOSIAH 20:11

They were not half so numerous as the Lamanites. **But they fought for their lives, and for their wives, and for their children**; therefore they exerted themselves and like dragons did they fight.

Before the young shepherd boy David went into the valley of Elah to face Goliath—a man twice as experienced and twice as big—he asked his brother the question, "Is there not a cause?" (1 Samuel 17:29). Even though reason said he shouldn't face the giant, David felt like there was a cause worth fighting for that couldn't be ignored. So he ran into battle.

When the people of Limhi were attacked by a Lamanite army that was twice as big as theirs, they ran into battle with a similar courage and with a similar cause—a cause they believed was worth fighting for. In their case, it was their wives and their families. The love they felt for them moved them to exert themselves and fight like dragons. Love gave them courage to do something hard. Love gave them courage to do something bigger than themselves. Love gave them courage to sacrifice.

When I read this story, I cannot help but think about Jesus walking into the battle with Satan, sin, and death. It seemed to be more than He could bear—perhaps the enemy appeared to be twice as big. But there was a cause worth fighting for. And that cause was love: love for His Father and love for us. Love gave Him courage and strength to fight and exert and endure until He was victorious. —DB

Reflect and Respond
What is worth fighting for in your life?

Your favorite scripture in Mosiah 20

MOSIAH 21:16

**And it came to pass that
they began to prosper by degrees.**

I once faced an illness I wasn't sure I would ever recover from. It was a devastating time. I longed for my health. What I wanted, more than anything else in the world, was to feel better. On one afternoon I called a good friend of mine who is a professional counselor. I told him I thought I might never get better. I explained how discouraged I was. He asked if I was making progress. I told him I was, but it was going so slowly.

He told me to pretend I had a truck and that I had taken a drive up into the mountains. When I got to the mountain, I got out of the truck and decided to hike up to the highest peak. I hiked and hiked for hours, but no matter how far I walked, it seemed I would never reach the destination. "That is exactly how I feel!" I told him, so happy that someone finally understood.

"Well," he said, "take a second to look back at the truck."

"What truck?" I asked him. I was so focused on the hike and the peak and the walking and walking for hours.

"The truck you parked at the bottom. It will tell you how far you have come."

I had totally forgotten about the truck. And sometimes we get so focused on the trial, the struggle, and the place we want to be, we forget to look back and see how far we have come.

It happened in the book of Mosiah to the people who were in bondage to the Lamanites. The scriptures tell us the Lord did not see fit to deliver them out of bondage; instead they began to prosper by degrees. Sometimes the miracle comes by degrees. In those moments, just pause for a minute and take a second to look back at the truck. —EBF

Reflect and Respond

Have you experienced a time when the Lord prospered you by degrees? What did you learn?

Your favorite scripture in Mosiah 21

MOSIAH 22:13-14

And after being many days in the wilderness they arrived in the land of Zarahemla, and joined Mosiah's people.... **And it came to pass that Mosiah received them with joy**.

Because of the choices of some of their leaders, the people of Limhi had been living in bondage to the Lamanites. They were taxed heavily and burdened with the sufferings of being slaves. They pled continually for the Lord to deliver them. Finally, He did. When they escaped, the Lamanites chased after them through the wilderness, but the people of Limhi had already arrived safely among the people of Mosiah. Even though they were strangers and came unexpectedly, and even though they might have deserved some of the struggles they were facing, King Mosiah and his people not only accepted them when they came but "received them with joy."

When I read this story, I think about all the excuses Mosiah and his people could have had to not accept the people of Limhi into their civilization. The people of Limhi had only what they could carry on their backs. They were refugees from another kingdom. Where would they live? Would they pay taxes? Would they burden the school, government, and health-care systems? Certainly Mosiah's people would need to be smart about managing this influx of people, but I love that the first detail that is mentioned with their arrival is that Mosiah, and presumably his people, received the newcomers with joy. Not with a cold shoulder or grudge or mistrust, but simply with joy. —DB

Reflect and Respond

What does it look like to receive others with joy? Do you know some "newcomers" who could receive this sort of acceptance?

Your favorite scripture in Mosiah 22

MOSIAH 23:28

Therefore they hushed their fears . . .

There was a time when the people of Alma were very frightened. The Lamanites were in the borders of the land. The people gathered together in the city, and they were afraid. "But Alma went forth and stood among them, and exhorted them that they should not be frightened, but that they should remember the Lord their God and he would deliver them. Therefore they hushed their fears" (Mosiah 23:27–28). Interestingly, things did not get better. In fact, they got worse! The people were led into bondage for a time. But they still trusted in the words of Alma and in the Lord, and they were not afraid.

I have been in situations when my heart has filled with fear. One, in particular, stands out. Honestly, it felt like all was lost. I remember my husband, Greg, asking me, "Where is your faith?" And I remember telling him, "I just don't have any more. You will have to have enough for both of us." And you know what? He did. My heart took courage from him.

Sometimes our fears are hushed by the faith of others who are strong enough to believe, to hold onto faith, to trust in God. In those moments we can lean on them until we are strong enough to stand on our own again. —EBF

Reflect and Respond

Describe a time when you have leaned on the faith and strength of another.

Your favorite scripture in Mosiah 23

MOSIAH 24:16

And it came to pass that so great was their faith and their patience that the voice of the Lord came unto them again, saying: Be of good comfort, **for on the morrow** I will deliver you out of bondage.

I absolutely do not like waiting for things. I don't like lines. Fast food is never fast enough. And counting down to holidays is the worst. I once celebrated Christmas five days early because I couldn't wait any longer for it to come. Patience is not one of my strengths. However, I have learned and experienced lessons in my life that can be learned only while waiting—particularly waiting on the Lord. One of the hurdles for me in waiting on Him is understanding that He has the power to do things quickly but sometimes chooses not to.

The people of Alma provide one example of a time when the Lord had the power to deliver but left them waiting. Even when he promised them rescue, He told them it would be "on the morrow." Why not right then? Why not that night? Often in our lives, we have to wait until the morrow before we experience, see, or recognize the Lord's blessings and miracles for us.

During these times of waiting in my own life, I have discovered that who we become while we wait is more important to Him than getting our answers or solutions right away. The trust we gain, the reliance on Him, the patience that grows, these are all blessings that come only as we wait until the morrow. —DB

Reflect and Respond

What blessings are you waiting on right now? What lessons are you learning as you wait?

Your favorite scripture in Mosiah 24

MOSIAH 25:10

When they thought of **the immediate goodness of God**,
... they did raise their voices and give thanks.

I am intrigued by the thought of the immediate goodness of God. As I read this verse, I assume that it means the most recent goodness of God, what just happened. It makes me question what the immediate goodness of God looks like in my life right now. When was the last time I recognized it? I have also started to realize that if I'm not taking the time to recognize it, I won't ever remember to give thanks for it.

So I sit down with a paper and pen and set my stopwatch for two minutes, intent on writing down every immediate goodness that comes to mind. I go through the names of each of my children and clearly see how God is blessing them, blessing their families. Things are hard, but God is there. The grandkids should each count as double goodness, every single one. The yellow Jeep. The opportunities I have to serve, and to teach, and to testify of Christ. Good friends. Projects I am passionate about. A weekend spent with family. *All immediate goodness.* I realize that I have remembered to thank God for some of those things, but not all of them. Some of the goodness has gone unnoticed.

I have decided to try something for this one week. Every night I am going to start my prayers by pondering on the immediate goodness of God. I want to recognize and remember all of it. And I want to give thanks. —EBF

Reflect and Respond

Set a stopwatch for two minutes and write down everything you consider as the immediate goodness of God. What did you discover?

Your favorite scripture in Mosiah 25

MOSIAH 26:26

And then shall they know that I am the Lord their God, that I am their Redeemer; **but they would not be redeemed**.

Picture in your mind a large ship out in the middle of the ocean that is sinking. Luckily, the captain has radioed for help, and plenty of lifeboats and helicopters arrive with capable and willing rescuers to save every soul on board. Could you imagine a person standing there on deck while the ship slowly dips into the water, refusing to climb into a lifeboat or grab onto the harness dangling from a helicopter? There is plenty of room and plenty of time to be rescued, but the person simply says no. It seems like an impossible scenario. Who would ever do that? It is hard to believe. That is how I feel every time I read this verse. My mind cannot catch hold of a reason why someone would choose not to be redeemed. I long for it so desperately that I cannot imagine that someone else wouldn't. In some cases it isn't ignorance or missed opportunity—it is a deliberate choice.

There will be some, for whatever reason, who will eventually come to know that Jesus is their Lord and their God—that He is both willing and able to rescue and redeem them—but who will choose not to receive that gift. Each of us is allowed to choose for ourselves whether we will be redeemed through the Savior's atoning grace. It is a gift that the Lord will not force on anyone, and we can receive it in any degree. He allows us and gives us the dignity of choosing for ourselves if we want Him to be our redeeming God. Consider where you are right now. How important is the gift to you? Would you choose to receive it? —DB

Reflect and Respond

How might you be refusing some of God's gifts of grace right now?
What can be done to allow them to flow more freely into your life?

Your favorite scripture in Mosiah 26

MOSIAH 27:14

Therefore, for this purpose have I come.

It is the moment when Alma the Younger is going about rebelling, the moment when the angel appears and asks Alma, "Why persecutest thou the church of God?" (Mosiah 27:13). Before Alma even has a chance to answer, the angel tells Alma the reason he has come: "Behold, the Lord hath heard the prayers of his people, and also the prayers of his servant, Alma, who is thy father" (Mosiah 27:14). The angel came because of the prayers of Alma's father, and surely of his mother and all the people in his community as well.

Have you ever wondered about the power of a prayer?

I am reminded of the story of a young boy who was struggling in high school. Things were so bad he moved away from home and into his grandparents' house for the summer. At the end of the summer a decision had to be made. Should he stay with his grandparents and attend a new school, or should he move back home and struggle against the friends who had pulled him down? His mom wanted him to stay; he wanted to come home. One afternoon she called to talk with him about the decision. She had prayed mightily before making the phone call that his heart would be softened, that he would know what to do. During the call, the boy came to his own conclusion, that it would be best for him to stay with his grandparents. The mother was astonished at how quickly his answer had come. She told him about her prayer before the conversation began, how she had prayed that, if necessary, an angel would come. "Mom," the boy quickly responded, "you were that angel." There is great power in the prayers of a parent. Of this, I am certain. —EBF

Reflect and Respond

Can you think of a time when you felt the power of your mother's or father's prayers? What did you learn?

Your favorite scripture in Mosiah 27

MOSIAH 28:7

And the Lord said unto Mosiah: Let them go up, **for many shall believe on their words**, and they shall have eternal life; and I will deliver thy sons out of the hands of the Lamanites.

A son received a mission call to serve for twenty-four months at the same time his mother received a cancer diagnosis and was expected to live eighteen to twenty-four months. Among everything else they were carrying and worrying about, one of the decisions the family was considering was whether he should leave to serve the Lord during such a difficult time. They were wise in understanding that there was no single correct answer for a situation like this.

Typical of their family, they turned to the Lord for guidance and strength. During these days of prayer, the son went to the temple to do baptisms for the dead. As he was standing in the water, the first name that came onto the screen was a person who had lived in a village right in the middle of the mission he had been called to. And so was the second name. And the third. And the fourth. He took this as a confirmation that the Lord wanted him to serve despite the situation at home. When he told his parents, they felt the same peace and assurance.

When I see King Mosiah struggling and praying and worrying about his sons going on their difficult missions, I see my friends' faces. And then I read the Lord's words to both of them: "Let them go . . . for many shall believe on their words, and they shall have eternal life; and I will deliver thy son . . ." And just like the sons of Mosiah, this son went too, and many heard and believed on his words. —DB

Reflect and Respond

What could go right in your family's life if you followed God's whispers despite the difficulties you face?

Your favorite scripture in Mosiah 28

MOSIAH 29:40

Yea, they did esteem him more than any other man . . . yea, exceedingly, beyond measure.

Many years ago, my father served as a mission president. The last advice he received from the Apostle who set him apart was to keep as many missionaries out on their missions as possible. Converting the missionary was as important as converting the people of California. My father took that to heart.

I recall more than one missionary living in our home while they worked through some of the particulars of their lives. They would accompany my dad throughout the day, whether it was to the mission office or to a conference somewhere in the mission. My dad wasn't just providing watchcare over these elders, he was mentoring them. They talked about the power of hard work, the disciplines of diligence, and the goodness of the gospel, and not just for a couple of days; it was for months. Before it was time for them to return home, each of those missionaries returned successfully back out to the field. My dad still keeps track of those elders today. Some have named their children after him. The power of his influence and his love changed lives.

When my dad returned home from that mission experience, his hair was gray and his suit hung large on his frame. I remember thinking he looked worn and weary as he stood at the pulpit for his last time with his name tag on. At the end of his message, he shared his testimony. I will never forget the fire burning in his eyes and the power in his voice as he declared: "Behold, I am a disciple of Jesus Christ, the Son of God. I have been called of him to declare his word among his people, that they might have everlasting life" (3 Nephi 5:13). I thought about the people who had been touched in some way by this disciple of Christ, my dad. I remember thinking I wanted to be a disciple like that. —EBF

Reflect and Respond

Is there someone you esteem more than any other man? Who is it?

Your favorite scripture in Mosiah 29

ALMA 1:30

They did not set their hearts upon riches;
therefore they were liberal to all.

In the dump in the middle of Tijuana there is a tiny church. Inside the church you will find a young Christian woman by the name of Brianna. She is in her early twenties. She came to the dump with her church group many years ago for a mission trip. After going back home she felt there was a work for her to do at that tiny church, so she returned and she is still there. It has been over four years.

Brianna taught herself Spanish by carrying around spiral notebooks and writing down the words she needed to know. She would practice them all during the day. It took six notebooks before she was fluent. She is the only person from the United States who lives at the small church in the dump. She is in charge of providing breakfast every morning. It is the only meal most of the people in the dump will eat each day.

There are almost 150 people who come to the church for breakfast every morning, and Brianna knows the name of every single one. She knows the children's names, too. She knows which mothers are expecting babies and when they will be due. She knows everything about everyone who walks through the doors.

It was on a humanitarian trip to Mexico that I met Brianna. I asked her how long she had been there, how she had learned Spanish, where she was from. Then I asked her how long she planned to stay. I will never forget her answer. "Every morning I pray to the Lord to ask if he needs me here today, and every day He says yes. When He says He doesn't need me here anymore I will go back home."

If you want to meet someone who hasn't set her heart on riches, go to the dump in Tijuana and ask to meet Bri. She will teach you what it means to give liberally to all. —EBF

Reflect and Respond

What is one way you could give liberally today?

Your favorite scripture in Alma 1

ALMA 2:11

Now the people of Amlici were distinguished by the
name of Amlici, being called Amlicites; and the remainder
were called Nephites, **or the people of God**.

There are so many different ways that we can identify ourselves and introduce ourselves based off of our jobs, our titles, our families, our nationalities, or any other number of factors. Who are you? I am a teacher. Who are you? I am an American. Who are you? I am a Butler.

In the beginning of the book of Alma, a man named Amlici rose in popularity and began a rebellion against the people and the government of the Nephites. Eventually, he proclaimed himself to be the king of the rebellion movement. The people who chose to follow him marked their foreheads with a marking and identified themselves as Amlicites. They wanted to be known as people who were connected with him—a man who stood in opposition to the Lord.

On the contrary, the remainder of the people—those who did not follow Amlici—were identified as Nephites, or the people of God. By this time in their history, the word *Nephite* was not so much a matter of who someone's ancestor was, but rather of their loyalty to the Lord. *Nephite* was a synonym for someone who wanted to be recognized as one of God's people.

I long for my name to mean the same thing. When people hear it, I would love if they considered it a synonym for a Christian or someone who loved and followed God. This is how I want to be remembered and how I want to be identified. I want someone to hear my name and think of Him. —DB

Reflect and Respond

*How and with whom have you chosen to identify yourself
with God?*

Your favorite
scripture in
Alma 2

ALMA 3:26

…according to the spirit which they listed to obey,
whether it be a good spirit or a bad one.

Many people have asked me if it was hard to take in the troubled boy who moved in with us many years ago. I always tell them it was. It was one of the hardest things we have ever done. If you asked Garett, he would tell you the same thing. Turning a life around is hard on everyone involved.

In those first months, every time we encountered a problem we would sit down and talk it through. I wish you could have heard some of those first conversations—why we don't punch people in our family, why we attend all of the meetings at church, why we show up on time for a job we have committed to. In the beginning these things were a struggle for him. Every time we would talk something through, he would tell me the same thing: "Mom, my bad spirits are fighting against my good spirits. I never know who is going to win." It was one of the best descriptions for temptation I have ever heard.

In those first days, the bad spirits fought against him every day. After a while it happened two or three times a week. Toward the end, it was mostly in his dreams that the conflict surfaced. He would wake up sweaty and wonder why those spirits wouldn't let him sleep. But he got good at recognizing the tactics of the adversary, and, more important, he learned how to strengthen his ability to listen and respond to the Spirit that was good. Learning the lesson has made him stronger, and he has filled his life with things that increase his ability to feel the Spirit because he believes, just as Alma did, "every man receiveth wages of him whom he listeth to obey" (Alma 3:27). —EBF

Reflect and Respond

What is one thing you do when you seek an increase of the Spirit in your life?

Your favorite scripture in Alma 3

ALMA 4:15

**... nevertheless the Spirit of the
Lord did not fail him.**

Do you ever have those times in your life when everything is going wrong? Why is it that struggles, trials, and the unexpected challenges of life seem to come in pairs, trios, and groups? In times like these, we often rely on something or someone sturdy and trustworthy to give us strength. But what if that falls apart too? What if it's our marriage or job or reputation that fails us?

Alma was the spiritual leader of a large group of people. He spent time encouraging them and inviting them to turn their lives over to the Lord. He made promises to them and prayed for them. Yet, at this time in his ministry, nothing was going right. Despite their decisions to be faithful, persecutions were piling up, afflictions were commonplace, and his people were being treated unfairly. In these sad moments, when Alma didn't know where to turn or where to direct the people to turn, he learned a powerful lesson. When everything else in life was unpredictable or uncertain, "the Spirit of the Lord did not fail him." He could rest in that truth.

With everything that could and does happen in the ever-changing world around us, one thing can remain constant—God. He will never walk away, will never leave us alone, and will never run out of time, patience, or strength. He will always be there. —DB

Reflect and Respond

Has there been a time when you have had to rely solely on the Lord for help or strength?

Your favorite scripture in Alma 4

ALMA 5:7, 9

Nevertheless, their souls were illuminated . . . and their souls did expand.

Alma 5 contains more than forty-seven questions meant to help us grow and progress. I love how Alma tells us in verse 62, "I speak by way of invitation." This chapter gives us an opportunity to perform a life assessment, to consider where we stand with God. In part of this life assessment we read about souls being illuminated and souls expanding, and we realize that this chapter gives us a chance to check the status of our souls.

The Prophet Joseph Smith was also interested in the status of our souls. In his sermon to the Relief Society given on April 28, 1842, Joseph Smith taught, "Don't be limited in your views with regard to your neighbors' virtues, but be limited towards your own virtues, and not think yourselves more righteous than others; you must *enlarge your souls* toward others if you would do like Jesus . . . as you increase in innocence and virtue, and you increase in goodness, *let your hearts expand*—let them be enlarged toward others . . . How precious are the souls of men!" ("Nauvoo Relief Society Minute Book," [39]; emphasis added; at josephsmithpapers.org).

Consider what both Alma and Joseph teach us about the importance and the condition of our souls. Alma invites us into experiences where our souls will be illuminated and expand. Joseph wants us to enlarge our souls and let our hearts expand. Theirs is an invitation for growth, for progression, for reaching the potential God has in mind for us, and their suggestions for growth include innocence, virtue, goodness, and the light of the everlasting word. It is a quest that is individual for each of us, but one that will bless us all, for, as Joseph reminded us, *how precious are the souls of men.* —EBF

Reflect and Respond

What is the status of your soul? When was the last time your soul was illuminated? When was the last time you felt your heart expand?

Your favorite scripture in Alma 5

ALMA 6:5-6

The children of God were commanded that they should gather themselves together oft, and **join in fasting and mighty prayer** in behalf of the welfare of the souls of those who knew not God.

On a trip to the Middle East, one of the things that was so enchanting and impressive to me was to hear the sounds of the call to prayer coming from all of the Muslim mosques. In their faith tradition, there are certain dedicated times of day when faithful Muslims will stop and pray. If they are able and want to, they will often gather together at the mosque to pray as a group. Each of the mosques has a sound recording of this invitation to come and pray, and it is played from speakers at these designated times. When there are several mosques in a city, the sounds come from all directions, bouncing off the walls, reminding everyone in the city it is time to gather for prayer.

There is something powerful about gathering together for prayer—to be united in hope, faith, and love for God and others. I love seeing a group of people bowing their heads both individually and collectively in moments like these. I love gathering as a family at the top of the stairs to plead together. I love saying "amen" after a Sunday morning prayer at sacrament meeting. There are feelings and experiences that are reserved and come only when a group gathers together in faith. This is one of the privileges of a faith community: to bring people to pray, to serve, and to love—and to invite others along.

—DB

Reflect and Respond

What memories do you have of powerful prayers that have taken place within a faith community?

Your favorite scripture in Alma 6

ALMA 7:7

Behold, there is one thing which
is of more importance than they all . . .

I remember a conference talk in which the President of the Church laid aside his notes to speak to the Saints. I don't remember that ever happening before or since. The prophet told us he would like to share with us "the *summum bonum* of it all," and then he shared a scripture found in Moroni 7:26 (see Gordon B. Hinckley, "Latter-day Saints in Very Deed," *Ensign*, November 1997). I was in high school at the time. President Gordon B. Hinckley was the prophet of my teenage years, and I was endeared to him. I listened with rapt attention to everything he said. I remember looking up the phrase *summum bonum* right after conference ended. It is a Latin expression meaning "the highest good." The most important. Above everything else. For some reason, President Hinckley felt Moroni 7:26 was the *summum bonum* or the highest good of it all. I studied that scripture until it became a part of me. I wanted to understand its importance the same way the prophet did.

When I read Alma 7:7, I am reminded of my President Hinckley experience. Alma said, " . . . there be many things to come; and behold, there is one thing which is of more importance than they all . . ." (Alma 7:7). The *summum bonum*. Then Alma bore his testimony of Jesus Christ who would come: a Redeemer who would "take upon him death, that he may loose the bands of death which bind his people; and he will take upon him their infirmities, that his bowels may be filled with mercy, according to the flesh, that he may know according to the flesh how to succor his people according to their infirmities. . . . And now behold, this is the testimony which is in me" (Alma 7:12–13). The *summum bonum*. The highest good of it all. —EBF

Reflect and Respond

Why do you think the knowledge that a Redeemer would come among the people was of more importance than anything else?

Your favorite scripture in Alma 7

ALMA 8:20

I know that thou art a holy prophet of God. . . . Therefore, go with me
into my house and I will impart unto thee of my food; and **I know
that thou wilt be a blessing unto me and my house**.

When my mom was a little girl, she grew up in a family that would not be considered one of the strong, active families in their church. Her parents were of mixed faiths, they had their hidden struggles, and they were battling along in life just like the rest of us. When President Spencer W. Kimball went down to Houston for a stake conference, he asked the leaders in the area for a recommendation of a family that he could visit while he was there. He didn't want to go to the bishop's or stake president's home, but rather to a family that would be a little unexpected. He decided to visit my mom and her family with another member of the Quorum of the Twelve Apostles.

When they walked in the front door, a feeling moved through my mom's little-girl heart like lightning. She knew in an instant there was something different about these people. The life of her family changed because of a feeling and faith she has passed on to the next generation, and it is still being passed on.

When Amulek met the prophet Alma, he invited him to his home because he knew the prophet would be a blessing to him and his house. A similar, perpetual blessing like the one that came to my mom took place because of another prophet's visit in another place. Simple invitations and simple interactions with a prophet of God can have generational impacts. —DB

Reflect and Respond

How have the prophet and his words been a blessing to you and your house?

Your favorite
scripture in
Alma 8

ALMA 9:17

**At some period of time they will
be brought to believe.**

Maybe it is a friend. Perhaps your mother. It might be your sons, or one of your grandchildren. Each of us knows someone who has let go of his or her belief. Time has taught me that the process of believing is an individual journey, and as much as we want to tell others how they should believe, we can't. Belief is gained through experience. Personal experience. It is unique to every individual.

The verse above is one of my most favorite scriptures because I know people who have let go of their belief. Taken a break. Walked away. I have learned the importance of respecting their journey. Learning to love for the sake of love. Setting aside agendas to simply be present in someone's life. It is not my job to suggest what those people should believe or when they should believe or why they should believe. Those are all answers I learned in a very personal way, on my own individual journey. I believe the same will be true for them.

But I also believe in the power of the counsel given at the end of this verse, "For the Lord will be merciful unto all who call on his name" (Alma 9:17). I am one of those who is calling on His name in behalf of those I love. I want them to know Him. I want them to feel His blessings in their lives. But I want them to discover that faith for themselves, in the way He has designed for them. I know He will be merciful. I know His patience is greater than mine. I know He has a plan for every one of His children. I trust that His plan is good and so is His timing. Because of that, I am content to believe. —EBF

Reflect and Respond

Take some time to pray today for someone whose decisions weigh heavy on your heart. Then put your trust in Him.

Your favorite
scripture in
Alma 9

ALMA 10:6

Nevertheless, I did harden my heart, for I was
called many times and I would not hear; therefore **I knew
concerning these things, yet I would not know**.

The poet Elizabeth Barrett Browning once wrote: "Earth's crammed with heaven, And every common bush afire with God; But only he who sees, takes off his shoes; The rest sit round it and pluck blackberries."

We find out from Amulek's story that he was a man who had wealth, influence, and lots of family and friends in the community. People to see, places to go—full schedule, but not necessarily a full heart. He told Alma that he was called many times by the Lord, tapped on the shoulder for a chance to listen, but he never heard. *He knew, but would not know.* He could see, but never really saw. All around him, God was blessing his life, but he never took the time to acknowledge Him. God was trying to speak to him, but Amulek never took off his shoes in reverence and gratitude—instead he just kept picking blackberries.

Perhaps he was too busy. Perhaps he didn't think he needed God. Perhaps he thought meaning came from things like bank accounts, followers, and busyness. It wasn't until he looked back that he realized that God had been there all along, consistently and patiently inviting him to a better and higher way of life. His awareness was what was lacking. And once he chose to hear, see, and know, it made all the difference. Meaning and purpose came spilling into his heart and life. God became a central figure in His life story. —DB

Reflect and Respond

What is God trying to say to you? What is He trying to invite you to experience? What do you know but choose not to know?

Your favorite
scripture in
Alma 10

ALMA 11:44

Every thing shall be restored
to its perfect frame.

One of my most favorite possessions is a 1975 pale yellow Jeep. Her license plate says *DAIZY,* and that is what I call her. She was restored by an old man in Nephi who wore faded blue overalls the day I picked her up to bring her home. Her steering wheel is on the right side. Her five-gallon gas tank is strapped into the back with a brown leather belt. There is nothing that brings me more joy in the summer than taking her out for a ride.

I think that is why I love the thought of the restoration Alma talks about in Alma 11:44. It will come to all. Nothing shall be lost. Everything shall be restored to its perfect frame. My friend who is blind will see. My son will no longer rely upon man-made insulin. My sister will hold her tiny son, Myles, once again in her arms.

That is what true restoration looks like.

I think how happy I am on a summer afternoon when DAIZY and I are driving home from an errand, and I realize that such joy can't even compare to what God holds in store.

In that day there will be a great gathering, unlike any we have experienced before: "Even so shall the covenant wherewith he hath covenanted with the house of Jacob be fulfilled in his own due time, unto the restoring all the house of Jacob unto the knowledge of the covenant that he hath covenanted with them. And then shall they know their Redeemer, who is Jesus Christ, the Son of God" (3 Nephi 5:25–26). —EBF

Reflect and Respond
Why does the knowledge of a restoration bring you hope and joy?

Your favorite scripture in Alma 11

ALMA 12:7

Now when Alma had spoken these words, Zeezrom began to tremble more exceedingly, for he **was convinced more and more of the power of God**.

Last summer, our family went through a large cave high in the mountains near our house. One of the things this particular cave is known for is its collection of stalactites and stalagmites that are everywhere inside. These impressive structures are formed by particles of sediment that drip with water and slowly build up over thousands of years. Some of them were massive and filled entire rooms inside the cave system. Others were just starting. It was intriguing to me that the largest structures were formed just like the small ones were—by small rock particles settling drip by drip by drip, consistently over all of those years.

Sometimes, people can pinpoint a moment when they feel like they became a believer or received a testimony—there is a story associated with the day they knew that God was real or that the Book of Mormon was true. However, this has not been the case with me. I relate more to Zeezrom's story—each day, week, month, and year I find myself "convinced more and more of the power of God." Like a slowly forming stalactite, my experiences trusting and recognizing the Lord have been building up, settling, and forming into my foundation of faith. An answered prayer here, a sense of peace there, a tender mercy on this day or that—drip by drip, I have become more and more convinced.

I might be able to pinpoint certain experiences that have been an important part of my faith story, but they are stronger when they are a part of a larger collection of moments that confirm my faith. —DB

Reflect and Respond

Can you list some of these moments that have convinced you more and more of God's power?

Your favorite scripture in Alma 12

ALMA 13:25

Would to God that it might be in my day;
but let it be sooner or later, in it I will rejoice.

Our good friend Nish once had a mentor with whom she would meet every Friday to study scripture. The woman lived in a home with a window looking out upon the grandeur of the Rockies. Hers was a home where you didn't knock, you just walked in. So, every Friday Nish would walk into the house, and she would find the woman standing at the window in her family room holding a mug in one hand but drinking in the beauty from outside. She would turn around when she heard Nish enter the room and welcome her with the same two-word greeting every single time: "Maybe today."

After several weeks, Nish asked her what it meant.

She learned that her friend stood at the window and wished for the coming of Christ. Every morning. When she turned away from the window, she expressed the anticipation and hope she always carried in her heart . . . maybe today.

Don't you love her hope in the coming of Christ?

Someday Jesus Christ will come again bringing deliverance, and unity, and love. He will come with healing in His wings to rescue, and restore, and reclaim. It will be a time of great joy and gathering. Would to God that it would be in our lifetime.

Maybe even today. —EBF

Reflect and Respond

What is it about the Second Coming of Christ that brings you the most hope and anticipation?

Your favorite scripture in Alma 13

ALMA 14:14

When the bodies of those who had been cast into the fire were consumed, . . . the chief judge of the land came and stood before Alma and Amulek, . . . and said unto them: After what ye have seen, **will ye preach again unto this people** . . . ?

When my wife, Jenny, was a missionary in Korea, she met a young college-aged woman and wanted to teach her the gospel. The woman agreed to listen because she felt like they were friends, but she told the missionaries that she could never and would never change religions. The cost would be too high.

During their first lesson, the missionaries taught her that she was an actual daughter of a Heavenly Father. The truth went into her soul like lightning and changed all her plans. When she decided she wanted to be baptized, some of her family members were furious. Her aunt kicked her out of the house she was living in, and she had to drop out of college. She lost friends, family members, and opportunities. Although it hurt, she knew she was doing what was right for her. She ended up using the money she had been saving for college to go serve as a full-time missionary herself.

I can hear the persecuting men's questions to Alma and Amulek come through time to this Korean girl. "After what you have seen, will you preach again?" When choosing God leads to trials and heartache and loss, will you still stay? Will you still testify of His goodness? —DB

Reflect and Respond

What difficulties have come into your life because you have chosen God? What helps you stay?

Your favorite scripture in Alma 14

ALMA 15:4

His heart began to take courage.

It is one of the best stories in the Book of Mormon: the story of a wicked man who had hoped to destroy two of God's best. Then he became sick with a burning fever, a fever that came because he supposed that the two men of God were dead. After some time, he heard that Alma and Amulek were actually in the land. Here are the two things we love about this story—first, his heart did take courage just knowing those two men were close by, and second, when he sent for the two men of God whom he had sought at one time to destroy, they came immediately.

When was the last time your heart took courage from men who were sent from God?

The first thing those two men asked the wicked man who lay sick in bed was, "Believest thou in the power of Christ?" He responded, "I believe all the words that thou hast taught," to which they replied, "If thou believest in the redemption of Christ thou canst be healed." And again, he replied, "I believe according to thy words" (Alma 15:6–9). Then the story ends with a prayer, and faith, and leaping, and a baptism. I love the leaping.

It all happened because two men didn't hold a grudge and one wicked man's heart took courage. It's a good story. It always is, when someone decides to believe. —EBF

Reflect and Respond

When was the last time your heart took courage from someone who was sent from God?

Your favorite scripture in Alma 15

ALMA 16:16

And there was no inequality among them; **the Lord did pour out his Spirit on all the face of the land** ... to prepare their hearts to receive the word which should be taught among them at the time of his coming.

One day I was in a random city in China walking down a street that was bursting with people. I passed by literally tens of thousands and perhaps more. As I squeezed through the crowds, I had a realization that the odds were very low that anyone in that city would ever come across the gospel of Jesus Christ during their lifetime. In fact, the number of people who will come across the fulness of the gospel while they live on the earth is remarkably close to 0 percent. These thoughts led to some bitterness. I was upset about how unfair it was. Why would they be passed over? Why was I one of the lucky ones? Then I felt a very distinct impression. A voice to my heart said, "I will take care of all of my children."

In the time of Alma and Amulek, the Lord was doing the same. There was no inequality among all of the people. He was pouring out His Spirit, in His own way and timing, upon all. Every single one.

Today people all over the world are still being prepared by Him to receive Him with gladness when He comes again. No one is forgotten or passed over. He will find a way to speak to every nation, kindred, tongue, and people and pour out His Spirit upon the whole human family. He is deeply concerned about and cares for everyone. —DB

Reflect and Respond

What are some ways that you see God pouring out His Spirit upon His children all over the world?

Your favorite scripture in Alma 16

ALMA 17:29

. . . win the hearts . . .

One of the best lessons on how to become a powerful teacher is taught by Ammon in the land of Ishmael. What is powerful about this lesson is how many things happen before Ammon actually opens his mouth to teach.

1. Ammon meets the king and asks to be his servant. (17:25)
2. He wants to win the hearts of his fellow-servants. (17:29)
3. His actions show he is a friend to the king. (18:3)
4. He feeds the horses. (18:9)
5. He prepares the chariots. (18:9)
6. He asks the king what he would have him do, and what he desires to know. (18:14)
7. *Finally*, he begins to teach. (18:24)
8. The king believes his words. (18:40)

There are sixty-two verses that pass by before Ammon does what he came there to do, to teach of Christ. It is a lesson that all teachers can learn from—and isn't that all of us? Before we teach a word, we must win the hearts and prepare the chariots. Maybe you wonder what that looks like in our day because most of us won't gather sheep, feed horses, or prepare chariots. The answer can be found in Alma 20:26, "And when he also saw the great love he had for his son Lamoni, he was astonished exceedingly." What made a difference wasn't the sheep or the horses or the chariots, it was the great love. There is a powerful message there. —EBF

Reflect and Respond

Think of the people you currently have an opportunity to teach.
What is one thing you could do to show great love?

Your favorite scripture in Alma 17

ALMA 18:35

And a portion of that Spirit dwelleth in me,
which giveth me knowledge, and also power according
to my faith and desires which are in God.

In 2017, in the United States, there was a solar eclipse. In the place where I was living, the sun was going to be covered about 95 percent. Four hours away from where I lived were places where the sun was covered 100 percent. I figured it wasn't worth the drive, so I stuck around. As the moment of eclipse got closer and closer, the area I was in was electric. Everyone was waiting with such bubbling anticipation. There was a countdown like it was New Year's Eve. And then it happened, and honestly, it wasn't that impressive. We took a quick picture and went on with our day. Later that night, I saw videos from some friends who had driven the four hours to see the 100 percent coverage. I couldn't believe it. The temperature dropped significantly; it went so dark they could see the stars. The difference that only 5 percent of the sun made was astonishing. I was so shocked that such a small percentage of the sun could still light the earth and keep it warm the way it did.

When Ammon was a missionary, he told the king that just a portion of the Lord's Spirit dwelt in him—and it gave him power and strength to do the miraculous. Just a portion. In such a grander way than the sun, but similar in analogy, just a portion of the goodness and presence of God has the power to change everything. And to have it, all we need to do is want it. —DB

Reflect and Respond

What are some things you can do to enjoy a portion of the Lord's Spirit today?

Your favorite scripture in Alma 18

ALMA 19:29

And as soon as she touched her hand
she arose and stood upon her feet, and cried
with a loud voice, saying: O blessed Jesus . . .

One of the best stories of ministering in the Book of Mormon takes place between two of the most unexpected women. One was a queen; the other was her servant. It is an unlikely friendship, but one that can teach us what it looks like to love well.

Abish was a Lamanite woman who had been converted because of a remarkable vision of her father. She was a woman who recognized the power of God. In hopes that others would believe in the power of God, she ran from house to house telling the people to come. Once they all arrived, things did not go as she had planned. There was contention and arguing. Fear had come upon them all. In that moment, Abish did the only thing she could think of—she took the queen by the hand with the hope of lifting her. As soon as she touched her, the queen arose and bore her witness of Jesus Christ.

We can learn several lessons from this story of Abish. In order to minister with power, we must first believe in God. Then we must have a desire to share that knowledge with others. In a moment of confusion and fear, the greatest desire of Abish was to lift the queen. I am reminded of a quote from Sister Becky Craven, "We are about elevating others" ("Careful versus Casual," *Ensign*, May 2019). The powerful lesson taught by Abish is a truth that is still relevant today. It is important to lift those we minister to. It is within the sharing of God's power and the deliberate lifting that others come to know and love the Lord. —EBF

Reflect and Respond

How could you apply the lessons of Abish to your ministering? How could you share the power of God? How could you lift?

Your favorite scripture in Alma 19

ALMA 20:26

And when he saw that Ammon had no desire to destroy him, **and when he also saw the great love he had for his son Lamoni**, he was astonished exceedingly.

I have a friend who was away from his faith for many, many years but happily, eventually came back. One day while a group of us were sitting around listening to his account of his journey, another friend asked, "What truth was it that made you want to come back? What drew you back to the Lord?" He shared several stories and gave meaningful examples, but his answer to the question was just one word: *love*. People loved him just as he was, and that was it.

When Ammon met the father of his newly converted friend King Lamoni on the roadside, they had a violent encounter. Lamoni's father was furious and beside himself. In his anger, he tried to strike his own son with a sword, but Ammon stood in the way to defend Lamoni. That act of love was powerful enough to derail the king from his current path and melt his severely hardened heart. He was astonished. Just because of love, the father granted Lamoni and Ammon all of their wishes and more. Just because of love.

Policy, arguments, and doctrinal dissertations didn't change these men's hearts—love did. And what if that were our only motive? What if we truly loved people for the sake of loving people? We know love can change a heart—imagine how it could change the world. —DB

Reflect and Respond
What can you do to express this type of love to someone today?

Your favorite scripture in Alma 20

ALMA 21:23

And he did exhort them daily, **with all diligence**;
and they gave heed unto his word, and they were zealous . . .

When our son Garett was looking into Division One schools where he might play football, we had an opportunity to meet with the defensive coordinator at the University of Utah, Morgan Scalley. He asked Garett what kind of football player he was: an orange eater, a gamer, or a doer. I remember how we all looked at him in confusion waiting for the understanding to come.

First, he described the orange eater. It's the person on the team who is most interested in the treat at halftime. He isn't interested in what is happening on or off the field; he is interested in the oranges.

Next, he described the gamer. The gamer is only interested in the game itself. He doesn't focus on what is happening off the field. He barely makes practice. He gives only what he has to until it's game time. Then he gives everything he's got. But because he didn't put the effort in at practice, he is never as good as he could have been.

The last is a doer. This is a player who is diligent on and off the field. He is first to the practice and the last one off the field. He takes more pages of notes than anyone else. He watches more film. He runs an extra mile. He spends extra time meeting with the coach. He is diligent outside of game time, and his diligence pays off. He is an athlete.

Ammon was a doer. He understood what it meant to be diligent and zealous toward what he was passionate about. When he arrived at the palace of King Lamoni he prepared chariots, and protected sheep, and won hearts (see Alma 17–18). His enthusiasm was contagious, and others were strengthened because of his passion for what was right. —EBF

Reflect and Respond
Where could you show more diligence?

Your favorite scripture in Alma 21

ALMA 22:15, 18

What shall I do that I may have this eternal life . . . ? Behold, said he, **I will give up all that I possess**, yea, I will forsake my kingdom, that I may receive this great joy. . . . I will give away all my sins to know thee.

It is incredible to imagine that the Lamanite king who was willing to give away half of his kingdom to know God was the same king who days before had tried to kill his own son for hanging out with a Nephite missionary. What a change!

All of us have probably said we would "give anything" to have or experience something else. I wonder how true this actually is. What are those things in my life that I would give anything for? I don't think the list is very long. In fact, even though there are things that I know should be on the list, I still sit here and wonder if I really mean it. What would I actually give?

In the first part of the conversation, the king told Aaron he would give half of his kingdom to receive the joy of eternal life. When the king knelt down in prayer—when he spoke, perhaps for the first time, to his own King—he promised something different. This time he offered all of his sins. Not just half anymore. And not just land and money. But this time, all of his heart. And for what exchange? To know God.

It is as Elder Bruce C. Hafen has said, "We can have eternal life if we want it, but only if there is *nothing else* we want more" ("The Atonement: All for All," *Ensign*, May 2004; emphasis in original). —DB

Reflect and Respond

In what way can you give your heart in exchange for knowing God?

Your favorite scripture in Alma 22

ALMA 23:6

. . . never did fall away.

In the book of Alma we learn of a group of people named the Anti-Nephi-Lehies. What is most fascinating about this group is that once they were converted to the Lord, they never fell away. "And as sure as the Lord liveth, so sure as many as believed, or as many as were brought to the knowledge of the truth, . . . and were converted unto the Lord, never did fall away" (Alma 23:6).

The first time I read that verse, I wondered if it was really true. After reading through the Book of Mormon several more times, I found and gathered other verses that confirmed the truth of it. Later in Alma we read, "And they were among the people of Nephi, and also numbered among the people who were of the church of God. And they were also distinguished for their zeal towards God, and also towards men; for they were perfectly honest and upright in all things; and they were firm in the faith of Christ, *even unto the end*" (Alma 27:27; emphasis added). This verse helps us to recognize qualities that allowed those people to stay converted to the gospel.

Last, we read in 3 Nephi 6:14, "In the thirtieth year the church was broken up in all the land save it were among a few of the Lamanites who were converted unto the true faith; and they would not depart from it, for they were firm, and steadfast, and immovable, willing with all diligence to keep the commandments of the Lord."

I want to live my life as someone who never did fall away, which means I must live with a zeal towards God, be firm in the faith of Christ, firm, and steadfast, and immovable. Never falling away requires effort *even unto the end.* —EBF

Reflect and Respond

What attributes in these verses do you think would help someone stay converted?

Your favorite scripture in Alma 23

ALMA 24:16

Behold, we will hide away our swords, yea, **even we will bury them deep in the earth**, that they may be kept bright, as a testimony that we have never used them, at the last day.

Sometimes when you pass a store window you see the phrase "Everything must go." This sign usually means there is a huge sale and the store is trying to get rid of inventory. One of the reasons a store wants to clear out some of its products is because they are no longer profitable. So the store owners sell them off so they can make room on their shelves for more profitable products. Everything that is not profitable must go to make room for the better things.

I think this is the same call we hear from the Lord. Everything must go. And why? Because He has something better in store for us.

The people of Anti-Nephi-Lehi who buried their swords deep in the ground understood this principle. They had rebellion on their shelves. They had violence taking up room. They had hatred and bitterness and grudges. But then they learned of things that are more profitable to the soul. So they buried the old to make room for the new. And they didn't just bury those old things—they buried them deep in the earth so they wouldn't dig them back up again the next week. They let them go. —DB

Reflect and Respond

When you hear the phrase everything must go, *what does your heart tell you it is time to get rid of? And what will take its place?*

Your favorite scripture in Alma 24

ALMA 25:17

... seeing that the Lord had granted unto them according
to their prayers, and that he had also **verified his
word unto them in every particular**.

It was my best friend's wedding. After several hard years, happiness had finally come. This was an important day, a long-awaited celebration. I wouldn't have missed it for the world, except there was an accident on the freeway. I was stuck in traffic. There was a good chance I wouldn't make the wedding.

It was long before cell phones, and I had no way of telling my friend the trouble I was in. I knew she would worry. I prayed the whole way to downtown Salt Lake City, *Please let me make it in time.* As I got off the exit, I immediately prayed for something I knew was not realistic, *Please let me find front-row parking at the temple.* If there was a spot there, I would make it. I turned the corner onto North Temple and drove east. Sitting at the light just before the gate of the entrance to the temple, I watched a car pull out of the spot closest to the temple gate. I couldn't believe my eyes. I prayed the whole time the light was red that no one would take that spot; miraculously, no one did. The light turned green, and I pulled into the very closest spot to the temple gate. Front-row parking. I made it to the wedding.

Over the last two decades, I have passed that parking spot hundreds of times. It has never been vacant since that day. Every time I drive by, I think to myself how the Lord hears our prayers, how He knows the particulars of our lives, and how in His own time and in His own way He is able to orchestrate miracles in our behalf. —EBF

Reflect and Respond
When has the Lord answered one of your prayers in every particular?

Your favorite
scripture in
Alma 25

ALMA 26:16

Behold, who can glory too much in the Lord? Yea, who can say too much of his great power, and of his mercy, and of his long-suffering towards the children of men? Behold, I say unto you, **I cannot say the smallest part which I feel**.

Once in a fast and testimony meeting, a woman came to the pulpit two separate times to share her witness. She stood up the first time during the beginning of the meeting to share her love and belief in God and His saving Son. As the meeting went on, there were longer pauses and breaks of silence between testimonies. Longer than usual. To end one of those pauses, this sister stood up again to share more of what was in her heart. She had recently moved to our ward from another country, and she told us when she got up to the pulpit (the second time) that in her ward or branch back home, you had to stand in a line if you wanted a chance to share your testimony. There were weeks when she wanted to share, but there were so many others who beat her to the front, she wouldn't get a chance. So, she said, when she saw a chance open up again here, she decided to take another one because "who can glory too much in the Lord? Yes, who can say too much of his great power, and of his mercy?"

Isn't that the truth? Could we ever run out of praises for our God? Is there a threshold we reach of too much? I agree with Ammon—"I cannot say the smallest part which I feel." —DB

Reflect and Respond

What can you do today to show your praise and love for God's goodness?

Your favorite scripture in Alma 26

ALMA 27:4

**. . . for they were treated as though they
were angels sent from God.**

Ammon's heart broke when he saw the destruction and warfare among the people he had come to love so dearly. He had come among them as an imperfect, flawed, normal, repentant sinner desiring to share the good news of Christ's mercy. They had treated him like he was an angel sent directly from the presence of God. Moments of shared faith had knit their hearts together, Ammon with love toward them and their hearts in love toward him. This happens when the gospel and its miracles are shared between two individuals or groups of people.

My brother and sister-in-law just returned from a trip to South America, where my brother served as a missionary many years ago. One night when they were there, they sent a picture to our family group-text chain of my brother embracing a man to whom he had taught the gospel when he was a young missionary. Most pictures tell a thousand words—this one told a million. Their tight grasp on each other, the smile in their eyes, and the tears on cheeks told a story of a normal, imperfect, repentant sinner who had been treated as an angel by a humble father and his family when he brought the good news of Jesus to that home. And now their hearts will always be filled with compassion for each other. Knit together. Because of the gifts that each of them gave to the other. —DB

Reflect and Respond

Whom do you consider to be an angel sent from God because of what they have brought you?

Your favorite
scripture in
Alma 27

ALMA 28:14

And thus we see **the great call of diligence of men to labor in the vineyards of the Lord**; and thus we see the great reason of . . . sorrow because of death and destruction among men, and joy because of the light of Christ unto life.

At the end of a terrible battle, as Mormon looked back and reminisced over the loss of life, he mourned that so many had died without a knowledge of God or because of their hatred for those who believed. But Mormon also rejoiced knowing that so many others had received the chance to know of the light and life that can be found in Christ. So much joy on one end, and so much sorrow that could have been avoided on the other. And so, from the dust, that great prophet sent out a call of diligence to labor in the vineyards of the Lord for the souls of men.

One of the most persecuted Christians in modern times, William Booth, was called before his monarch, King Edward VII, at the end of his life because the king wanted to recognize him for all the good he had done for the world despite the mounting attacks against him. The king asked him to sign his autograph book. The elderly man hobbled forward and scribbled out the following:

> *Some men's ambition is art.*
> *Some men's ambition is fame.*
> *Some men's ambition is gold.*
> *My ambition is the souls of men.*
> (Cyril Barnes, *Words of William Booth* [1975], 72)

This is the call of the Lord that so many have answered—to labor in the vineyard, to fight for the souls of men. —DB

Reflect and Respond

Who do you know who has the ambition to labor for the souls of men? What can you learn from them?

Your favorite scripture in Alma 28

ALMA 29:9

. . . and this is my joy.

In this chapter, Alma considers four powerful thoughts in relation to the work God has in mind for him. First, "I ought to be content with the things which the Lord hath allotted unto me" (Alma 29:3). Second, "I know he granteth unto men according to their desire" (Alma 29:4). Third, "Why should I desire more than to perform the work to which I have been called?" (Alma 29:6). And last, "Perhaps I may be an instrument in the hands of God" (Alma 29:9).

It is an interesting thought process, and one I have found myself asking at different seasons of my life, particularly when I am caught up in the direction someone else's life is moving in. In those moments of comparison, I wonder if the Lord would say to each of us, "Be content with what you have and who you are. Align your desires with my desires for you. I have a work for you to do. Ask to be an instrument in my hands. Let me use you how I will."

What if we woke up every morning prepared to go through that thought process as we scheduled out the day? What would be the result? Alma gives us the answer: "And this is my joy" (Alma 29:9).

Our greatest joys will come from being an instrument in His hands to bring others to Him. The Lord has given us just what we need in order to do His work. If we fill our hearts with the desire to perform the work He has in mind for us, miracles will happen—and then, how great will be our joy. —EBF

Reflect and Respond

Are you content with what the Lord has given you? What is your greatest desire? What is the Lord's desire for you?

Your favorite scripture in Alma 29

ALMA 30:40

And now what evidence have ye that there is no God, or that Christ cometh not? I say unto you that ye have none, save it be your word only.

When Korihor, an anti-Christ from the time of Alma, came to the prophet, he demanded proof for the existence of God. Instead of immediately answering, Alma first shifted the burden of proof back onto Korihor. Why does a believer have to prove the existence of God to others? Why don't nonbelievers take the challenge instead to prove that He doesn't exist? Alma might not have been able to provide proof of the reality of God, but he didn't think Korihor could provide evidence of the contrary. In fact, Alma went on to say that everything he saw was a witness of God. If Korihor wanted to prove there was no God, he would have a lot of explaining to do. Alma pointed to the stars, planets, sun, and seasons and everything around him and said they all testified of a Creator.

Have you ever gazed into a starlit night sky, or marveled at a sunset, or stood in awe at the rhythmic crashing of waves dictated by tides? Have you ever considered that an entire continent of forest is packaged up in a tiny seed? Do you realize you have experienced these amazing scenes with eyes that supersede any camera ever invented and ears that capture invisible waves of sound and a heart that beats with emotion and life without any human assistance?

None of these observable wonders prove that God is real or behind the creation and orchestration of such a complicated life system on this planet, but the reality of them leads a person to consider it. And it quiets someone who has no proof against Him. —DB

Reflect and Respond
What wonders of creation inspire you to believe more in God?

Your favorite scripture in Alma 30

ALMA 31:5

The preaching of the word had a great tendency to lead the people to do that which was just—yea, **it had had more powerful effect upon the minds of the people than . . . anything else**.

When I look back at the hardest times of my life, one thing is consistent. For every hard moment, I found a scripture to cling to until the time had passed. Over the course of my life, I have collected these scripture verses. I consider them close friends that have helped carry me through hard times. Some of my favorites are Isaiah 43:1–5, Matthew 11:28–30, D&C 128:22, and 2 Chronicles 20:20. Elder Ronald A. Rasband has called verses like this "protection scriptures." He suggests that all of us should have a protection scripture we can cling to during a time of great need (see "Jesus Christ is the Answer," Evening with a General Authority, February 8, 2019).

During one seminary lesson I shared Elder Rasband's invitation with my class. My students decided to begin collecting a list of protection scriptures. Here are some of our favorites:

Deuteronomy 31:6	Matthew 7:7	Enos 1:8	D&C 6:36
2 Samuel 22:2–3	Mark 5:36	Mosiah 2:41	D&C 11:28
2 Chronicles 20:15	John 6:38	Helaman 5:12	D&C 50:24
Psalm 4:1	1 Corinthians 13:11	Helaman 12:23	D&C 63:47
Psalm 5:11	Galatians 2:20	Moroni 7:19	D&C 109:22
Micah 7:8	2 Nephi 4:20	D&C 4	D&C 121:7
Matthew 5:38–48	2 Nephi 4:26	D&C 6:13	
Matthew 6:25	2 Nephi 31:20	D&C 6:34	

Perhaps they will become some of your favorites. God's word is powerful. It can guide us, comfort us, and give us protection. In most circumstances, His words can have a more powerful effect than anything else. —EBF

Reflect and Respond

Begin collecting your own list of protection scriptures. What would your first one be?

Your favorite scripture in Alma 31

_____

_____

ALMA 32:27

Even if you can no more than **desire to believe**,
let this desire work in you, even until ye believe.

In my scriptures next to this verse there are four words written: "prepare a landing place." They are simple, but they cause me to stop and ponder every time. What would it look like to prepare a landing place?

When my children were young, they loved to grow a garden. We had a large patch of ground in our backyard that was planned just for that purpose. But just because we had dedicated it as the garden spot didn't mean it was ready once spring came. Actually, it was always a disaster in the spring. Every year when I walked out to inspect the area, I would notice three things: the ground was hard, the weeds had already taken root, and there were always rocks in the way. It didn't matter how careful we had been the year before, we always had to begin again every single spring. We would bring in a tiller, pull out all the rocks that had risen to the surface over the long winter, and pull out all the weeds. We would hoe the rows for the water lines and fertilize the soil. One whole evening was always devoted to getting the garden ready—to preparing a landing place.

The next evening, we would bring out the seeds. Because the soil had been prepared, the seeds were ready to thrive. In fact, the process of planting seeds was easier because we had already prepared a landing place.

One of the ways we can prepare a landing place in our hearts is to desire to believe and then remove the distractions or whatever might get in the way. Doing this will help us to prepare a landing place for God's word to grow. —EBF

Reflect and Respond

What can you do today to prepare a landing place for God's word to grow?

Your favorite scripture in Alma 32

ALMA 33:16

. . . because of thy Son . . .

I was once talking with a friend who asked me why I do all the things I do. He was talking about my ministering assignments, my seminary teaching, and my Church calling on top of the regular day-to-day activities of my life. As he is not a member of The Church of Jesus Christ of Latter-day Saints, his confusion made sense; from the outside it would look like I had taken on a lot of extracurricular assignments. I tried to think of a good answer for explaining all of the activities I had taken on, and the thought that immediately came to mind was, *because Jesus.* It was an overly simplified answer, but true. I do everything I do because of Him. Because I love Him. It's that simple.

The prophet Zenock taught a similar truth. He was speaking of a group of people who disbelieved on the Son of God. Zenock spoke to God, saying, "Thou art angry, O Lord, with this people, because they will not understand thy mercies which thou hast bestowed upon them *because of thy Son*" (Alma 33:16, emphasis added). I can't help but ponder on the mercies that have come into my life because of His Son. Not just a few, so many that I can't even number them. The truth of it makes me stop to ponder. What if I were to look back over the past twenty-four hours, over the past week, over the past year? What if I were to look at the whole lifetime of each of my children? What if I were to consider my profession, my friendships, the place where I live? How much of it came *because of His Son,* through His mercies? *Because Jesus.* —EBF

Reflect and Respond

When was the last time you stopped to consider the mercies that have come into your life because of the Son?

Your favorite scripture in
Alma 33

_____

ALMA 34:18-29

Yea, cry unto him . . .

Whenever I wonder if something is appropriate to pray for, I turn to Alma 34:18–29. I would write down all the words of those verses here, but you have probably read them enough times that they are already familiar to you. Instead, I want to write down what I hear when I read them. It sounds something like this: Cry unto Him over your work and over your husband's profession. Cry unto Him for each of your children, and their spouses, and your grandchildren. It's okay to plead to Him for all of those people, everyone under your roof, and don't worry if you don't get it all right the first time, you can cry unto Him three times a day because He cares about all of those people just like you do. Cry unto Him to help you overcome whatever you are up against today—deadlines, people you struggle with, people who are against you. Cry unto Him against the powers of the adversary—doubt, discouragement, fear. Don't let Satan talk you out of achieving God's righteous desires for you. Cry unto Him over your projects and tasks, whatever they may be, that you will do your best with them. Cry over your ideas and your creations, that they may increase. Pour out your soul wherever you happen to be—in your everyday places, in your hidden heartache places, in your wilderness places. And when you don't have time to cry out, just turn your heart to Him all day long for whatever you are in need of, and for the needs of whoever is by you. And while you are asking Him to take care of you and your needs, remember to look outside of yourself and take care of others around you. That is most often how He answers our prayers, through the actions of someone whose heart is turned to Him but whose arms are outstretched to all. —EBF

Reflect and Respond

Read Alma 34:18–29. What do you need to cry unto Him for today?

Your favorite scripture in Alma 34

ALMA 35:9

And they did administer unto them according to their wants.

Every time I read this story, I wonder if I would be able to love like the people of Ammon did. When Alma and Amulek's converts were cast out by the Zoramites because their hearts had been changed, they came to the people of Ammon begging for safety and a place to stay. The people of Ammon did not cast them out; they nourished them, and clothed them, and gave them a place to live. They didn't just take care of their needs, they ministered to them "according to their wants" (Alma 35:9). It sounds so nice when we read it, but it is not an easy thing to do.

When we were very first married, Greg was called as the Young Men president in our tiny ward. It was a married student ward, and all of us were in college, so there were only a few boys in the Young Men program. Greg was in charge of planning the first camping trip. It went well, and by that I mean no one died. A few weeks after the camp, I was in our storage room. I noticed that the tent and the sleeping bags and camp chairs we had received as a wedding present were missing. "What happened to our camping gear?" I asked him when he got home from work. "I gave it away," he replied simply. "What?" I asked, a little bit heated. "We haven't even used it yet!"

"Exactly," he replied, wondering why it wasn't clear to me. "We haven't ever used it, and those boys have to go camping several more times this year. They need it more than we do."

It was an immediate lesson in our marriage that I had to quickly learn to accept. Greg will give away everything we own to anyone who needs it more than we do. He has a heart like the people of Ammon. I'm trying to learn to be more like him. —EBF

Reflect and Respond

Practice having a heart like the people of Ammon today. Recognize the needs of someone you are with and give unto them.

Your favorite scripture in Alma 35

ALMA 36:22

Yea, methought I saw, even as our father Lehi saw, God sitting upon his throne, surrounded with numberless concourses of angels, in the attitude of singing and praising their God; yea, **and my soul did long to be there**.

I have a friend who served in the armed services, and while he was overseas, he was unable to be a part of several family and friend activities. He missed reunions, baptisms, the birth of a baby, and every holiday and tradition his family had during that time. Every now and then, he was able to Skype home and see his family gathered around the screen. When those video chats ended with "I love yous" and little hands blowing kisses, his heart always said what Alma said so many years ago—*my soul did long to be there*. For him, home was a vision of heaven, and he wished more than anything that he could be there too.

One of the most powerful parts of Alma's longing is what he said just before telling the story of his mighty change. He told his son that because of his guilt and sins, "the very thought of coming into the presence of my God did rack my soul with inexpressible horror" (Alma 36:14). Once he learned the true nature of God and felt the grace and forgiveness of the Savior, he went from running away from the Lord to a heart yearning to run toward Him.

Perhaps if we feel like the old Alma, uncomfortable with the thought of being in His presence, then we have something more to learn about who He truly is and how all-encompassing His mercy can be. When we come to truly know Him, our hearts will long to be with Him. —DB

Reflect and Respond

Why does your soul long for heaven and for God? What are the blessings you hope for and look forward to?

Your favorite scripture in Alma 36

ALMA 37:36

Cry unto God for all thy support; **yea, let all thy doings be unto the Lord**, and whithersoever thou goest let it be in the Lord; yea, let all thy thoughts be directed unto the Lord.

Every time I read this scripture in Alma 37, I am reminded of a favorite scripture in Proverbs 3:5–6: "Trust in the Lord with all thine heart; and lean not unto thine own understanding. In all thy ways acknowledge him, and he shall direct thy paths."

Matching scriptures.

I love when that happens.

When I find repetition in the scriptures, it makes me think that the Lord must want to make sure we didn't miss it the first time. But just in case we did, He repeats it so that we are sure to understand. I always think to myself, *this must be an important principle if He took the time to mention it twice.*

Here is what stands out to me from these verses. The Lord has not left us to walk through this journey alone. We don't have to figure everything out by ourselves. As we recognize Him, cry unto Him for support, and trust Him, then He will direct our paths, and wherever we go, it will be in the Lord.

It is a beautiful promise. It is the best way to travel through life. —EBF

Reflect and Respond

Mark both of these verses in your scriptures and put a link to each of them. How could you let Him direct your path today?

Your favorite scripture in Alma 37

ALMA 38:12

Use boldness, but not overbearance.

Before I left home for a full-time mission, my mom collected letters from family members who wanted to give me advice. My sister told me not to eat any dog meat, and my cousin asked me to be on the lookout for Pokémon cards written in Korean. They could be valuable someday. I treasured all the advice I received, particularly from my family members who were older and had more life experience with loving and serving and helping other people.

Alma 38 is a similar advice-giving conversation between the prophet-missionary Alma and his son Helaman, who would also hold that same responsibility and mantle. One thing he told Helaman was to be bold but not overbearing. I wish I could sit down with him and have him give me examples of what he means, but I bet he would tell me the advice I already know—*feel it out*. On one end, we cannot let the fear of being overbearing keep us from courage. I could hide behind the second part of the advice and never open my mouth. On the other end, I could take boldness too far and offend and even hurt relationships, all in the name of Christlike courage and boldness. Rudeness and unrighteous zeal can never be dressed up and pass as boldness.

Perhaps Alma himself didn't expound on that advice with his son because there are no formulas for striking the right balance. Every person is different, and we need to approach each of them as such. People are not experiments or equations, they are human souls, and the Spirit knows just the right amount of boldness for each. —DB

Reflect and Respond

Is there a place in your life that needs a little more boldness? Are there other places where tenderness would be more fitting?

Your favorite scripture in Alma 38

ALMA 39:10

**Take it upon you to counsel with your elder
brothers in your undertakings.**

This is the advice of a father to one of his sons who was struggling: a boy who needed to change his ways. To turn away from some things and turn back to others. He gave him the advice you would imagine: refrain from your iniquities, turn to the Lord, acknowledge your faults. But there was one thing more: "Take it upon you to counsel with your elder brothers in your undertakings; for behold, thou art in thy youth, and ye stand in need to be nourished by your brothers. And give heed to their counsel" (Alma 39:10). Go talk to your brothers. Ask them what to do. Get their advice. Listen to their counsel.

I've watched my own kids do this over and over again. There were many nights one of them would wait for another on the front porch late, after their dates, to talk before they walked into the house. I've listened in on the phone call of the one who just suffered a great disappointment calling another to find out how they got through a similar situation years before. I see them writing emails for advice on missions, calling for advice on girls, asking about financial choices. And sometimes, when one of the kids calls for advice about something I am just not sure about, I will respond, "Call Josh," or "Call Megan," or "Call Garett," they will know what to do. Go talk to them. Ask them what to do. Get their advice. Listen to their counsel.

It has made our family stronger, this relying on each other. It's helped us through times of struggle and disappointment, and even times of great joy. We turn to each other first. And that has made all the difference. —EBF

Reflect and Respond

Call a brother or sister for advice today. Let them know how much you appreciate them.

Your favorite
scripture in
Alma 39

ALMA 40:3

Now, I unfold unto you a mystery; nevertheless, there are many mysteries which are kept, that no one knoweth them save God himself. **But I show unto you one thing which I have inquired diligently of God that I might know** . . .

I once heard an interview with a man who said he had so many questions about faith and God when he was growing up. One day, while asking his religious leader some of those questions, the leader responded by saying, "Good little boys don't ask questions like that." That answer turned him off from asking and eventually turned him off from faith. Interestingly, they go hand in hand. Faith is born out of an inquisitive mind.

Alma was talking to a son who was worried and had questions about truth and doctrine—especially about the next life. As Alma spoke with his son, he taught him that we do not have the answer to many mysteries about God. However, he was able to share one mystery because it was one that God had shared with him. We get a little peek into Alma's past in the process of learning that mystery when he said, "I show unto you one thing which I have inquired diligently of God that I might know." Then a little later he said, "the thing which I have inquired diligently of the Lord to know . . . this is the thing of which I do know" (Alma 40:9).

I wonder what it looked like for Alma to inquire diligently. I am also intrigued that his mind and heart were focused on learning one truth but he still was at peace with others he did not have answers to. The Lord loves an inquiring mind—and He counsels us that diligence, not just curiosity, leads to answers. —DB

Reflect and Respond

What is your "one thing" that you are inquiring diligently to know right now?

Your favorite scripture in Alma 40

ALMA 41:14

Do good continually . . .

Every time I call my sister on the phone, the conversation begins the same way. I say, "How are you doing?" and she says, "Doing good."

And most of the time, she is. Literally.

She is always *doing* good.

It is her nature to see a need and fill it, to love first, to give. She will put aside anything to help someone in need. It's who she is.

I'll never forget a time almost three decades ago when she was running for an office in junior high. A special education teacher asked one of her students who he was voting for. "Oh! Sara!" he replied enthusiastically. He didn't even have to think about it. "Why?" the teacher wondered at his immediate choice. "Because she loves everyone," he replied sincerely, "even people like me."

It is the best description of her I have ever heard: she loves everyone. She really does. And because her heart is so full of love, her life is filled to the brim with doing good continually. She reminds me of a favorite scripture in Acts 10:38, speaking of Jesus, "who went about doing good." Maybe we could all try to be a little more like that. —EBF

Reflect and Respond

Try doing good continually today. Write down what you experience.

Your favorite scripture in Alma 41

ALMA 42:30

**Let the justice of God, and his mercy, and
his long-suffering have full sway in your heart.**

To discover what motivated me, someone once shared an analogy with me that went like this: If you were in a rowboat in a steadily moving stream, what would get you to row against the current? The fact that downstream there is a waterfall that crashes onto rocks and will lead to certain death, or the fact that upstream there is a city of gold that waits with all the luxuries you would ever want? Are you more motivated by avoiding the waterfall or by getting to the golden city? Which would you choose? Which one motivates you more? Perhaps it is a combination of both.

As Alma was talking to his son who had made some heartbreaking decisions, he told him that he wanted three things to have full sway on his heart, to motivate and move him—the justice of God, the mercy of God, and the long-suffering of God. Perhaps, in the analogy, the waterfall could symbolize God's justice and the golden city could be His mercy. Maybe both of them would motivate you. That is probably true. One thing that is powerful about Alma's advice is that he does not want justice, mercy, and long-suffering to motivate his son, but rather the justice, mercy, and long-suffering *of God* to motivate him. These are not arbitrary ideas or lifeless concepts; they are the doings and feelings and emotions of a life-giving God. As we allow justice and mercy to have full sway on our hearts, we also get to allow God's patience, His long-suffering, to have an impact on us. He doesn't care how long it takes us to get there; He just cares that we do. —DB

Reflect and Respond

Think about justice, mercy, and long-suffering. How do you allow them to have sway in your heart right now?

Your favorite scripture in Alma 42

ALMA 43:30

**He thought it no sin that he should
defend them by stratagem.**

Many years ago, we went camping with our family. All of the kids were in Grandma Bonnie's trailer waiting for breakfast to be ready. Greg and I were outside when all of a sudden we heard screaming from inside the trailer. There was complete silence for one minute, and then the screaming began again. Greg and I took off running for the trailer, opened the door, and tried to assess the situation. By the time we got there, all was silence. My brother-in-law and all the kids were sitting on the couch staring transfixed at the oven door, which was closed. Grandma Bonnie had dropped her mug on the floor, spilling its contents everywhere, and she too was standing transfixed, staring at the oven door.

"What happened?" Greg yelled, and everyone turned to look at him. "Fire came out of the oven!" my brother-in-law replied, still shell-shocked. "Twice. The door opened and a fireball shot out, then it closed, then it opened again, and another fireball shot out, and then it closed again." Next came the most important question from Greg, "Why are you all still sitting on the couch?" he asked incredulously. "I don't know," my brother-in-law replied. "We didn't think about running out."

In that moment I realized how important it is to decide what you would do before you get into a situation that could be dangerous. So later that morning we held a family council and decided if you ever see fire in a trailer, the smartest thing to do is run out. But we also learned from the principle and talked about what to do in other situations as well. What if someone offers you drugs? What if a friend encourages you to shoplift? What if you end up in a place you shouldn't be? How could you get out? A previously planned strategy can make all the difference when trouble comes. —EBF

Reflect and Respond

Consider some rough situations you might have to face in the future. What should your strategy be?

Your favorite scripture in
Alma 43

ALMA 44:3

But now, ye behold that the Lord is with us.... **And now ye see that ye cannot destroy this our faith**.

An unknown poet once wrote:

All the water in the world,
However hard it tried,
Could never sink the smallest ship
Unless it [gets] inside.
And all the evil in the world,
The blackest kind of sin,
Can never hurt you the least bit
Unless you let it in.
(*Best-Loved Poems of the LDS People*, ed. Jack M. Lyon and others [1996], 302)

Sometimes we might feel like we are that little ship far from the safety of shore, surrounded by all the water in the world. We might look around and feel threatened, ever on the edge of being attacked and overcome. Much like our common enemy, the devil, Captain Moroni's mortal enemy, Zerahemnah, was unrelenting and persistent in seeking to ruin and destroy the people of God. I love Moroni's bold declaration to him—*You cannot destroy our faith*.

Faith is a decision that we get to make and choose to hold on to. No attack or argument or adversary can ever destroy it unless we give it up. And in the words of that mighty captain, the reason we cannot be destroyed is because we have the Lord with us—the Captain of our souls. Our Captain will not let evil in. He gives us authority and courage to look our enemies in the eyes and tell them they have no place here. They are not welcome here. They have no power here. —DB

Reflect and Respond

In the moments when your faith is being questioned, attacked, or undermined, what will you say to the enemy of your soul?

Your favorite scripture in Alma 44

ALMA 45:1

And they did worship God with exceedingly great joy.

I learned a new meaning of *worship* when I visited the Holy Land a while back. Our trip began in Jordan, and while we were there I heard the call to prayer five times a day. I saw people pause at dawn, in the early afternoon, late afternoon, and at sunset, to step away from the everyday to kneel and worship Allah. In the middle of the night I would hear the call to prayer, and I woke and said my own prayer because I wanted to experience that type of worship.

When we arrived in Jerusalem, it was the Sabbath. I watched the women light the Sabbath candles; I watched the flames dance back and forth, spreading joyful light. I brought home two candlesticks because I wanted to experience that type of worship.

When we were in Egypt, I heard about a whirling dervish. The dervishes worship God through individual experiences, one of which is a whirling dance. On our last night we had the opportunity to witness a performance of this religious dance performed as an expression of love for God. I sat transfixed through the performance because I have always wanted to experience that type of worship.

People worship in many different ways, and I have found that learning to appreciate the way someone else worships often strengthens our own belief. My friend Michael Wilcox calls it "holy envy." It is the practice of honoring someone else's devoted worship.

What I found true about each of these forms of worship is that they brought each individual great joy. Perhaps the best way to worship, or reverence, or serve God is to do it with exceedingly great joy. For each of us it might look different. Some will pray, some will light candles, some will dance, but in the end all will worship with exceedingly great joy. —EBF

....

Reflect and Respond
How is your worship joyful?

Your favorite scripture in Alma 45

ALMA 46:15

And those who did belong to the church were faithful;
yea, all those who were true believers in Christ **took
upon them, gladly, the name of Christ**.

When I sat down in my Algebra II class in high school, the first thing the girl next to me told me was that I was not a Christian. I usually begin with introductions, but instead I responded that I considered myself one and asked her to define a Christian. She replied, "A person who believes in Christ." I said back, "Guilty as charged." To which she rebutted, "A Christian is someone who believes in Christ and reads the Bible." Again, I said, "Guilty. Two for two." She sighed an exaggerated sigh and then said, "A Christian is someone who believes in Christ, reads the Bible, and doesn't read any other book, especially the Book of Mormon." At that point I caved. I suppose according to that particular definition I was not a Christian. But I actually prefer Mormon's definition of what a Christian is, as found in the Book of Mormon. In narrating the story of the people about to go to war against the Lamanites, Mormon gave the group a name—the band of Christians—and then he gave three defining attributes of those people. First, they were "true believers of Christ." Second, they were "faithful" to Him. And third, they "took upon them, gladly, the name of Christ."

That is the Book of Mormon definition of a Christian, as given by Mormon himself. Ironically, the definition is contained in the book that seemingly disqualifies those who read it as Christians by others who call themselves by that very name. Despite how others may define me, I yearn to be described the way that Mormon talked about that band of Christians so many years ago. I would hope to be counted as one of them. —DB

Reflect and Respond

Are you a true believer in Christ? Are you faithful and loyal to Him? And how do you gladly take on His name?

Your favorite scripture in Alma 46

ALMA 47:18

Amalickiah caused that one of his servants
should administer **poison by degrees**.

Every time I read the story of Lehonti and Amalickiah, I find myself talking out loud to my scriptures. In the first half of the chapter I spend my time encouraging Lehonti, "Don't come down! Not even a little bit! Stay where you are!" He never listens. He always comes down. It's because Amalickiah comes nearly to Lehonti's camp, and when it seems like the distance is not too great, Lehonti comes down.

It's just the beginning of the problems ahead, because the next thing that happens is that Lehonti is poisoned by degrees. Note how similar Amalickiah's tactics are—come down *just a little,* and then he poisons him *by degrees.* It is how Satan works: a little at a time, and by degrees.

It is an interesting lesson because most of us probably wouldn't purposely enter a situation that we knew would put us in great danger. But going just a little bit out of our comfort zone, tolerating wickedness in small degrees, for some reason just doesn't feel as dangerous. And so the adversary leads us down the path, making us comfortable slowly, until we are entangled in his web.

Instead of coming down a little and accepting wickedness by degrees, we will benefit by obeying the Lord's counsel to stand in holy places and be not moved. There we find safety. There we find strength. —EBF

Reflect and Respond

What are some ways you have learned to stand in holy places and be not moved?

Your favorite
scripture in
Alma 47

ALMA 48:9

And in their weakest fortifications he did place
the greater number of men; **and thus he did
fortify and strengthen the land**.

Anticipating an attack from their enemies, Chief Captain Moroni fortified and strengthened the Nephite cities against a worst-case scenario situation. Interestingly, and wisely, he strategically placed greater numbers of men in the spots that he considered the weakest. As a strapping, young, rising military star, Moroni might have felt tempted to avoid or ignore the fact that his cities had weak spots. Perhaps weak spots reflected weakness in the leader. Instead, he saw those potential dangers, and instead of puffing himself up in pride or being naïve about their reality, he did something about them—and it made all the difference in the war.

Recently, a close friend of mine confided in me about a temptation and struggle he was battling. I am certain it was not easy to bring up the topic, and it certainly wasn't an enjoyable conversation for either of us to have. He risked being judged, looked down upon, and seen as weak. In order to save face and avoid risk, he could have ignored the weakness or pretended it wasn't there. Instead, he gathered people he trusted around that spot—a "greater number"—to stand guard and to watch over him. His courage is inspiring. His wisdom is supreme. His humility gave him great strength. It will make all the difference in the war. —DB

Reflect and Respond

How can you gather people to your weakest places for strength?

Your favorite
scripture in
Alma 48

ALMA 49:14

The city . . . which had hitherto been a weak place,
had now . . . become strong.

It is a promise found throughout scripture.
- "My strength is made perfect in weakness." (2 Corinthians 12:9)
- "Therefore I take pleasure in infirmities, . . . for when I am weak, then am I strong." (2 Corinthians 12:10)
- " . . . out of weakness were made strong . . ." (Hebrews 11:34)
- "And out of weakness he shall be made strong . . ." (2 Nephi 3:13)
- " . . . then will I make weak things become strong unto them." (Ether 12:27)

Although we see it in so many places, I particularly love the lesson we are taught in Alma. The city that once was weak was now strong for many reasons. First, Moroni had appointed one of his strongest captains, Lehi, to stand guard there, and the enemy feared Lehi exceedingly. But Moroni had also encouraged the people to build up the banks; he prepared them with stones and arrows; and a body of their strongest men stood ready.

The lesson we learn from this is powerful. A weak place never has to remain weak. The Lord has promised over and over again that He has the capacity to strengthen us. How will it happen? Through righteous leaders, through hard work, through preparation, through surrounding ourselves with strong people, and through His grace. It doesn't matter what our weak place is, the Lord will help to make us strong. —EBF

Reflect and Respond
Which of the tactics described above would help you to find strength in your weakness?

Your favorite scripture in Alma 49

ALMA 50:23

But behold **there never was a happier time** among the people
of Nephi, since the days of Nephi, than in the days of Moroni.

If you were to pull this verse out of the pages of the Book of Mormon and didn't tell me the context and surrounding verses, I never in a hundred years would guess that it was a description of the people directly in the middle of the war chapters—one of the most devastating and heartbreaking parts of their history. They were not just described as happy, but comparatively, there "never was a happier time" among the people. What is it about ransacked cities, mass graves, and bloodthirsty enemies encroaching upon you that leads to happiness?

Similarly, I have always loved the description Patty Sessions, an early pioneer who crossed the plains of Iowa alongside Brigham Young, gave of that very prophet leader who went along with them. First, you should know that some of the most difficult crossing points for the early pioneers were in Iowa. The mud was so thick they had to double-team each of the wagons. They would hook up two sets of oxen to one wagon to pull it through a spot of mud, and then unhook them, walk them back to the other wagon, hook up both sets to that one, and pull the wagon to meet up with the first. Then, repeat over and over again. All the way through Iowa! In those conditions, Patty Sessions said, "Brother Brigham came up with his company driving his team in mud to his knees as happy as a king" ("Journal of Patty Sessions," 12 Feb. 1846, typescript, Church History Library).

In mud. In war. There can be happiness. —DB

Reflect and Respond

What advice about finding happiness would you give to someone in the middle of battle?

Your favorite scripture in Alma 50

ALMA 51:16

For **it was his first care** to put an end to such
contentions and dissensions among the people.

When my boys were young, they used to fight all the time over everything. Toys, who got the biggest piece of cake, what movie to watch on TV. I quickly learned to step in within the very first minute the contention and dissension started. If I stepped in at the beginning, I could mediate the situation, the problem would be resolved, and the day would continue in peace.

In those early years, keeping the Spirit in our home became my first care.

It is still true today.

When contention arises or I feel dissension enter a conversation, it is my first care to put an end to it and invite the Spirit to return.

President Russell M. Nelson counseled, "In coming days, it will not be possible to survive spiritually without the guiding, directing, comforting, and constant influence of the Holy Ghost" ("Revelation for the Church, Revelation for Our Lives," *Ensign*, May 2018). In order to have the constant influence of the Holy Ghost, we must learn to put an end to contention and dissension, which are some of the quickest ways to lose the Spirit.

It must become our first care. —EBF

Reflect and Respond
What could you do to put an end to contention and dissension?
How could it become your first care?

Your favorite
scripture in
Alma 51

ALMA 52:19

Moroni and Teancum and many of the chief captains
held a council of war—what they should do.

When my friend was called as a Relief Society president, she came over to the house for some ice cream and some advice. I had served as a member of the ward council for several years before, and it was her first time. Although I was confident she could have gone to several people more qualified to give her advice, I figured she came for the ice cream, and I simply passed on the advice I had received and lived by in previous years.

The first was to open my mouth. Revelation usually comes scattered and spread out through the group. In a council, if I didn't speak what came to my heart, the revelation would be incomplete or would need to come another way. The second piece of advice, similar to the first, was that I was there as a neighbor, parent, and community member first, and then in my particular calling second. My experiences mattered and were valuable to the council. In my years in that ward council, I watched revelation come to the group. I saw the hand of God moving and working through the messiness and majesty of a council willing and ready to speak up, listen, and love.

Like Moroni and Teancum, we are in a time of battle, a battle for the souls of men. Oftentimes, we don't know what to do. So we gather in councils in families, friend groups, neighborhoods, and churches to combine the experience and wisdom of many in order to learn and hear what to do. I am certain such councils contributed to the victory in the Nephite wars. I am a witness it led to victory many times in my life. The same can be true in yours. —DB

Reflect and Respond

What councils do you or could you bring together to learn what to do in your life situations?

Your favorite scripture in Alma 52

ALMA 53:20

And they were all young men, and they were **exceedingly valiant for courage, and also for strength and activity**; but behold, this was not all—they were men who were true at all times in whatsoever thing they were entrusted.

Some of the best young men I know approached me one afternoon to see if we could do a Bible study once a week throughout the entire summer. They determined it would be held on Tuesday nights for two hours. I agreed and then wondered how many would actually come. They were high schoolers. It was summer. To my surprise, they all did. Every Tuesday night for the whole summer. They picked the topics they wanted to study, they led the discussions, they brought their scriptures and notebooks to write in. I was the moderator and in charge of pointing them in the direction they should go to look for answers. We started a text group and sent quotes and insights back and forth during the week. *What in the world? Who does that?* Four boys and one girl who were determined to prepare for their missions. They didn't miss a week.

Now they are all out on those missions. One is in the Philippines, two are in California, one is in North Carolina, and the last is in Canada. They are speaking Chinese and Spanish, Cebuano and English. Every time I read their letters, I think about how we used to sit around on summer nights and talk about verses in the scriptures, and how they are teaching those same scriptures to people all over the world.

The young people in this generation are so good. Exceedingly valiant for courage, strength, and activity. But this is not all, they are true at all times in whatever they are entrusted with. The Lord's finest. I wish you could invite some over to your backyard. —EBF

Reflect and Respond
Give a compliment to a young man or young woman you know.
Let them know how great you think they are!

Your favorite scripture in Alma 53

ALMA 54:12

And behold, if ye do not this, I will come against
you with my armies; yea, **even I will arm my women
and my children,** and I will come against you.

It thrills me that when Moroni sent a letter to Ammoron, leader of an enemy army set on destroying the Nephites, he tried to get Ammoron to surrender by warning him that he would come against him with his women and children. Under some circumstances, a man of war might not be very threatened by such a warning. But, as we see in later chapters, perhaps he should have been. It is especially true in ancient culture, but often enough even today, that women and children are overlooked and not seen as a strength, force, or contribution for good. This is a wildly unfortunate cultural tragedy. Underestimating or excluding the gifts and the spiritual capacity of women and also children is simply foolish.

During the first year of President Russell M. Nelson's ministry as the prophet and President of The Church of Jesus Christ of Latter-day Saints, he spoke to both the women and the youth in two separate meetings to invite them particularly and deliberately to become willing and anxious members of the Lord's battalion in these last days—and not just as a support to the men, but as independent, contributing soldiers for truth and righteousness.

"Tonight I urge you, with all the hope of my heart," he said, "to pray to understand your spiritual gifts—to cultivate, use, and expand them, even more than you ever have. You will change the world as you do so" ("Sisters' Participation in the Gathering of Israel," *Ensign*, November 2018). —DB

Reflect and Respond

*What has God armed you with? What gifts do you see in the women
and children you know that will help them change the world?*

Your favorite
scripture in
Alma 54

ALMA 55:32

For if their wine would **poison** a Lamanite it **would also poison** a Nephite; and thus they did try all their liquors.

This might seem like an odd verse for a devotional, but here is the lesson, and it's a good one—poison is poison. If it isn't safe for one person, then it isn't safe for another. So, if you don't think your kids should watch that movie, then it's probably not good for your soul either.

The way the Nephites avoided being harmed by the poison was simple: "[They] were not slow to remember the Lord their God in this their time of affliction. They could not be taken in their snares; yea, they would not partake of their wine, save they had first given to some of the Lamanite prisoners" (Alma 55:31). The antidote to poison is twofold: go through the process of determining if it is poison and stay close to the Lord.

It's simple but true. There are sites we shouldn't visit, movies we shouldn't see, friends we shouldn't hang around with, places we shouldn't go, and things we shouldn't partake of. For the most part we know what those things are. But some areas are gray; some things are more uncertain. That's when our relationship with the Lord becomes important. If we remember Him in those moments, He will help us know what to do.

Anything that resembles poison in any way should be considered poison. We should avoid it like the plague. Stay away from it. Leave it alone.

Instead we must find sources of protection. Create a stronghold. This is the way we will fortify our families. —EBF

Reflect and Respond

Do you have things in your life that could be considered poison?
How could turning to the Lord help you avoid them?

Your favorite scripture in Alma 55

ALMA 56:47

They did think more upon the liberty of their fathers than they did
upon their lives; yea, **they had been taught by their mothers**,
that if they did not doubt, God would deliver them.

As we go places and people see our kids, they say things like, "Oh, you have your mother's eyes!" or, "You are the spitting image of your dad—wow!" Once, when one of our babies was born, someone who came to the hospital said, "That baby is a perfect mix of the two of you!" Truthfully, all of my kids probably want less of me in them, but what kids get from their parents isn't exclusively genetic or how they look.

The 2,000 stripling heroes we know and love from the Book of Mormon are so admirable in part because of what they inherited and learned from their parents. I love the credit Helaman gives the boys' mothers, who taught them never to doubt, to look to God for strength. Their righteous courage was passed on to their sons. Helaman also told us that the young men thought about the liberty of their fathers more than their own lives. Remember, their fathers made covenants that they would never fight again, and it was important to these boys to help them keep those promises. Imagine also what it meant to them to see that their fathers would be willing to keep those promises.

Earlier in Helaman's letter, we learned that the fathers were the ones who brought provisions to their sons while they were in battle. They may have promised not to fight, but they were not going to stop giving their support in all ways they could.

Covenant-keeping fathers and righteous, courageous mothers make stripling warriors.
—DB

Reflect and Respond
In what ways have your father and mother shaped your faith?

Your favorite
scripture in
Alma 56

ALMA 57:6

We received a supply of provisions, ... **besides sixty of the sons of the Ammonites** who had come to join their brethren, my little band of two thousand. And now behold, we were strong.

The boy was three years old when he wandered away in the west desert of Utah and got lost. He was missing for days. Search parties were assembled. The army was called. Search and Rescue came with their dogs. All through the day they searched to no avail. In our neighborhood, a huge group gathered to drive down to the desert and help. They left in the afternoon. One man was late getting home from work. He missed the ride with all the others. He decided not to go. But his wife had packed his dinner and his stuff, and she had the car ready and waiting when he pulled in. So he went, even though he was late. When he arrived at the scene, everyone had already gone out searching. There was no one there to give directions, so he knelt and prayed, and then he went where the Spirit directed. There were thousands searching the desert that day. But the man who found the three -year-old boy was the one who almost didn't go—the one who showed up late.

When the Lord calls, it's never too late. When someone needs our help, sometimes showing up is more important than showing up on time. Such was the case in the story of the 2,000 stripling warriors. In Alma 57, sixty more boys showed up. They came to join the army. Late. We don't know why; we just know they came. I love what Helaman said after they arrived, "And *now* behold, we were strong" (Alma 57:6; emphasis added). Who needs you to show up today? —EBF

Reflect and Respond

When it is important, show up. Even if you are late. Bring your strength; God will provide the miracles.

Your favorite scripture in Alma 57

ALMA 58:37

But, behold, it mattereth not
—we trust God will deliver us.

When my mission president came to Korea, he brought three of his children with him who were still in school. The family was already feeling cultural whiplash from coming to a foreign country, but soon they learned that the barge bringing all of their things was delayed, and the international schools that had accepted their children's applications were now denying them admittance. Those first few days the parents went from the embassy to schools to city hall trying to figure out how to get their kids in school all while trying to serve in their new positions presiding over 180 missionaries. Their kids were nervous, hesitant to be there, and if they couldn't get the schooling worked out, they didn't know what they were going to do. Frustrated and overwhelmed, my mission president and his wife called the Area President. I will never forget what he said. After they explained all the problems and the potential disasters, he simply responded by quoting one scripture, Abraham 2:8: "My name is Jehovah, and I know the end from the beginning; therefore my hand shall be over thee."

And that is exactly what happened.

When Moroni was looking at his situation during a particularly tough part of the war, it might have looked like a total failure. The Nephites had lost cities to the Lamanites, women and children had been kidnapped, and the armies were receiving no help or support from the government. And yet, like the Area President in Korea, Moroni knew that whatever things looked like—it didn't matter. He would still trust in God. —DB

Reflect and Respond

What are some of the ways we can show our trust in God even and perhaps especially when things don't look like they are going right?

Your favorite scripture in Alma 58

ALMA 59:9

It was easier to keep the city from falling into
the hands of the Lamanites **than to retake it** from them.

When Abraham heard that Lot was taken captive, he armed the servants of his household, 318 men, and went to rescue him. It was Lot's own fault—he was the one who had faced his tent toward Sodom; he was the one who had eventually moved into the city. Because of the location he had chosen, he was in the wrong place at the wrong time, and he was taken captive. But Abraham still performed a rescue.

It can happen to any of us when we let down our guard. The first step doesn't feel that dangerous. Neither does the second, usually. It takes some time before we are in trouble. I love the principle Moroni teaches in this verse—it is easier to keep the city from falling than to retake it. It is true. But it doesn't always happen that way. In Abraham's case, no one knew there was a need for rescue until Lot had already fallen. In Moroni's case, not enough men showed up to keep the city.

Perhaps it is a lesson we can learn from. When someone is struggling, when there is a chance of falling, perhaps we could provide the increase of support in the beginning, to keep them, so we don't have to send 318 men to rescue them.

It doesn't mean the keeping will be easy. It will still require people, and fortification, and effort. But if it truly is easier than the retaking, then let us focus every effort on that.
—EBF

Reflect and Respond

*Do you know someone who is falling? What could you do to help
"keep" them?*

Your favorite
scripture in
Alma 59

ALMA 60:23

Now I would that ye should remember that God has
said that **the inward vessel shall be cleansed** first,
and then shall the outer vessel be cleansed also.

While we were getting our house ready to put up on the market and sell, we spent a lot of time getting the outside of the place looking as clean and crisp as possible. We power washed the siding and windows, bought a new welcome mat, painted the front door, filled the front flower beds with new dirt, and put bright new pillows on the porch bench. Our realtor told us houses that have great curb appeal and look good on the outside generally sell better.

While all of this was great advice for selling the house, it is terrible spiritual advice. In fact, the Lord's advice is quite opposite. Cleanse the inner vessel first, and "then shall the outer vessel be cleansed also."

Eventually, those who came to look at our house before buying had to walk around inside—they opened drawers and cupboards and became very familiar with the house. Spiritually, no one sees what is going on inside of us, and because all anyone knows is what they see on the outside, we can be tempted to neglect our intentions, desires, and thoughts at the expense of making sure we look good and righteous in our appearance. We will always be concerned with the outward. It is natural. But if we make it our first priority, we will easily neglect the inward—the part of us that matters most. —DB

Reflect and Respond

What are some of the inward things of your soul that need cleansing?

Your favorite scripture in Alma 60

ALMA 61:9

I . . . do rejoice in the greatness of your heart.

Not long ago, my friend went through a bad breakup with a lot of disappointment. It was just before Valentine's Day. It looked to be the worst Valentine's ever. He woke up feeling so sad and discouraged. Then the Spirit whispered, *There are people sadder than you today. Think of how many people won't receive any flowers.* My friend didn't take the prompting for granted. He went out and bought flowers, and for the remainder of Valentine's Day he delivered flowers to everyone he could think of who would be spending the day alone. At the end of the night, he showed up at his grandmother's house with the last flower in his hand. "What are you doing here?" she asked when she opened the door. "You should be out with your friends." He kissed her on the cheek and told her he loved her and didn't want her to have a Valentine's Day without any flowers. She looked up at him and said, "Your grandfather would be so proud." Now this has become his tradition; he does it every year. And when he gets married, he will do it with his wife. I just love the greatness of his heart. He shared that story with me two days before Valentine's Day this year, and I couldn't stop thinking about it. So that night our family delivered flowers to sixteen widows in our neighborhood. It was the best Valentine's Day ever. Now it is our tradition too.

Sometimes you meet people who have a greatness of heart. Learn from them. Listen to how they live their lives. Greatness has a way of overflowing, of spreading, of multiplying. If you spend enough time with them, your heart will become greater too. —EBF

Reflect and Respond
Who do you know who has a greatness of heart? What could you learn from them?

Your favorite scripture in Alma 61

ALMA 62:4-5

And he did **raise the standard** of liberty in
whatsoever place he did enter. . . . And it came to pass
that thousands did flock unto his standard.

Do you know someone who is the life of the party? When that person is there, the room feels a little more electric, people laugh more, and somehow he or she is able to pull people out of their shells. Every family and group of friends has that one person who everyone hopes is coming, who somehow knows how to work a crowd and light up the room wherever he or she goes.

I wonder if you know someone who is like that spiritually, someone who gives you strength when he or she is near, courage to be a little better, and has a spiritual presence that warms the soul. This is what I imagine Moroni was like. As he went from place to place, we learn that he raised the standard wherever he was. I love that Mormon chooses the word "raised" when talking about the standard of liberty. It makes we wonder what else was lifted or elevated or raised up with the flag each time Moroni came to a new place. Did their trust in God increase? Was their behavior on a higher level? Did their conversations seem more heavenly? Whatever it was, because of Moroni's influence, thousands flocked to the standard—a loyalty to defending God, family, and faith. People always knew it was what he stood for, and it inspired them to reach higher for the same.

—DB

Reflect and Respond

In what ways can you raise the faith and goodness of the groups
you associate with and places that you go?

Your favorite
scripture in
Alma 62

ALMA 63:13

Nevertheless, these things were to be **kept sacred, and handed down** from one generation to another.

When my grandmother died, we each got to pick something to remember her by. I chose two things—her scriptures and her scripture journal. I love those books. I keep them in my top drawer next to my bed. The notes in her scriptures are dated 1958. I love looking for the red markings in the verses she studied and reading her cursive script in the margin detailing what she was learning.

I am particularly fond of her journal. She linked scripture verses with stories. When I read it, I wonder if it is where she kept material for teaching. In the middle of the book there is a small piece of paper with a quote written in the cursive script I have come to know so well. It says, "Christianity can be lost in one generation if we do not teach our children." It reminds me of the verse at the end of Alma that talks about the plates being kept sacred and handed down from one generation to another, the same way I read from my grandmother's scriptures, and perhaps one day my children will read from mine. They will look at the markings and read the notes in the margins about what I was learning, and maybe our hearts will connect, and they will hold them sacred and keep them in the top drawer next to their bed, and they will remember. —EBF

Reflect and Respond

If there was something from the gospel you could hand down to your future generations, what would it be?

Your favorite scripture in Alma 63

_____

_____

HELAMAN 1:18

...for **they had supposed** that the Lamanites durst
not come into the heart of their lands.

Supposing can be a dangerous thing. Such was the case for Moronihah. He supposed the Lamanites would not dare to come into the center of the land to attack, but that they would attack from the borders. So Moronihah strengthened the borders and left the center weak and unprepared.

Sometimes evil enters into the heart of our cities and communities and families, giving us no time to gather or prepare, leaving us lost and wounded. But all is not lost. When unexpected trouble comes, when trials hit us at our very core, hopefully there are covenant people within reach. Strength in our borders. People to respond.

As soon as Moronihah realized what had happened, that evil had entered into the place he never would have supposed, he immediately sent for Lehi, and Lehi came. Lehi battled from one side and Moronihah from the other, and the Lamanites could not retreat either way, "neither on the north, nor on the south, nor on the east, nor on the west, for they were surrounded on every hand" (Helaman 1:31). When the war was over, Moronihah again took possession of the land.

The same is true for us. When the adversary hits the hearts of our families in a way we never would have supposed, we must reach out for assistance immediately and ask for covenant people to surround us on every side. Therein lies our strength, and that is how battles are won. —EBF

Reflect and Respond

Where would you turn for help if you found yourself facing a trial you never supposed would happen?

Your favorite scripture in Helaman 1

HELAMAN 2:13

In the end of this book ye shall see that this Gadianton did prove the overthrow, yea, **almost the entire destruction** of the people of Nephi.

Elder Dieter F. Uchtdorf once told a story about a sightseeing plane ride that ended in tragedy. The plane left New Zealand with more than 250 people on board for an exciting turnaround trip to fly over and see the breathtaking sights of the frozen and mountainous continent of Antarctica. When the pilots took off, they were unaware that their initial trajectory was off by a mere two degrees. However, by the time they neared their destination, it put them off by twenty-eight miles, and right in the path of an active volcano. The smoke from the billowing Mount Erebus blended with the clouds in the sky and the white on the ground, making the mountain practically invisible to the pilots. By the time the instruments in the plane sounded their warning, it was too late, and the crash ended in a total loss (see "A Matter of a Few Degrees," *Ensign*, May 2008). If only someone could have warned them at the beginning of the flight that this small two-degree error would end in a tragic crash.

When we are first introduced to Gadianton in the beginning of the book of Helaman, Mormon gives us as modern readers the end of that story as well. Because of this one man and the evil he put in motion, almost all of the people of Nephi would be destroyed. It is inspiring what good a single person can do, and it is also scary what one evil person can do. The people we choose to align with, the choices we make, and the direction we are facing, although those choices seem small at first, end with much larger consequences.
—DB

Reflect and Respond

Is there something in your life that needs adjusting, perhaps even by just two degrees?

Your favorite scripture in Helaman 2

HELAMAN 3:21

And it came to pass that he had two sons . . . and
they began **to grow up unto the Lord**.

When my daughter-in-law delivered her baby, she missed church for several weeks in a row. Not wanting to miss taking the sacrament, she asked if she could be on the list of people who had the sacrament delivered to their homes.

After church the priests arrived. They brought bread and water, a tray and cups, and knelt beside the table on the floor of our family room. We all gathered around for the sacred experience—the prayers, the taking of the bread and water, the remembering.

After it was done, we thanked the boys and walked them to the door. I returned to the family room just in time to watch my grandson Kingston, barely two years old, walking back into the room from the pantry with a slice of bread in his hand.

In silence we watched him break the bread into pieces and lay them carefully on the table. Then he knelt down, folded his arms, and bowed his head. There was silence for a time, and then he got up and handed each of us a piece of bread. It is one of the sweetest experiences I have ever witnessed.

I don't know how much Kingston understood about what took place in our family room that day as he sat on his mother's lap and watched, but I know he knew it was important. Sacred. That it had to do with broken bread, and bowed heads, and silent reverence. As I watched, I thought to myself how grateful I am that he is growing up unto the Lord. —EBF

Reflect and Respond

How have you watched a young child in the process of growing up unto the Lord? What does it teach you about your own journey?

Your favorite
scripture in
Helaman 3

HELAMAN 4:15

And it came to pass that they did repent, and **inasmuch as they did repent they did begin to prosper**.

I remember feeling so much anxiety, as I was growing up, about the word *repentance*. I saw it as a synonym for *punishment*. If anyone talked about it in church, I turned off my ears. In my mind, it was a painful, step-by-step process to walk through in order to receive forgiveness from the Lord. I thought it was associated with shame, disappointment, and guilt. The whole idea made me want to run and hide.

Once, while reading the book of Genesis, I felt like I was in good company. After Adam and Eve ate the forbidden fruit, they ran and hid from God too. When He came to the garden and called their names, I imagined Him calling my own. I thought to myself—why would I run and hide from the Lord? Why am I turning my back on the only one who can help me? Perhaps Adam and Eve felt the same, because eventually they came out from behind the tree.

That image of Adam and Eve coming back out from hiding into the protective presence of God became my new picture of repentance. Interestingly, the pain I had experienced came from poor decisions, not from the decision to repent. There is no punishment in repentance. There is consequence for sin, and the consequence of being left on our own because we turned away from Him. The word *repentance* implies a turning back, and turning back invites Him back into our lives. Then we begin to prosper. We prosper because He is there. We will never find the strength, love, and grace behind the tree that we will in His presence. Turn again to Him. —DB

Reflect and Respond

When have you experienced His presence and prosperity returning after you have turned again to Him?

Your favorite scripture in Helaman 4

HELAMAN 5:40

What shall we do, that **this cloud of darkness may be removed** from overshadowing us?

I have a friend who was going through a really hard time. When it became clear that the trial was not going to be removed anytime soon, he began to feel very discouraged. We went to lunch at the time and talked about the cloud of darkness that hung over his head. "I can't shake it," he told me. "It's always there." He asked what I do on my dark days. I gave him the best advice I could think of.

First, I have a certain playlist I turn to when life gets me down. The songs speak of hope, and healing, and Jesus. It's not a short playlist; every time I find a song that fits those three categories, I add it to the list. Listening to that music is a sure way to lift my heart.

Second, I pray. In fact, I pray extra on dark days, even if I don't feel like praying. I have learned to rest my burden on the Lord, to share it. To pour it out. There is peace that comes in the pouring out.

Last, I have a list of ten things that make me happy. I call it my ten essentials. They aren't necessarily spiritual things, although reading scriptures is on the list. But so are eating a cookie, going for a walk, buying flowers at the grocery store, spending time with Greg, taking a bubble bath, and reading an uplifting book for fifteen minutes.

"Try those three ideas," I told him. "See if it helps." You know what? He did. He tried it, and it worked. When the trial was finally over, he called to thank me for the three ideas and then he told me he was going to keep doing them—all of them—even though he doesn't necessarily believe in God. He liked how he felt when he prayed. —EBF

Reflect and Respond

What are your three things? What do you do when you want the cloud of darkness to be removed?

Your favorite scripture in Helaman 5

HELAMAN 6:1

Their righteousness did exceed that of the Nephites, **because of their firmness and their steadiness in the faith**.

I married a runner. Soon after we got married, we made a deal—if I ran one full 26.2-mile marathon, I would never have to do it again for the rest of my life. So I did it. Before I started training, the longest I had ever run was three miles. Each new distance was an accomplishment for me. On the day of the marathon, my grandpa gave me some advice: "Just put one foot in front of the other." I kind of laughed it off and headed up the canyon for the race. As simple as that advice was, I cannot tell you how many times I thought of it as I ran. But more important, I cannot tell you how many times I have thought of it since then. Just keep putting one foot in front of the other. Slow and steady.

Mormon's explanation for why the Lamanites were more righteous than the Nephites was categorized by two words—*firmness* and *steadiness*. It would be a compliment to be described as someone firm in the faith. It sounds like someone who is strong and committed, whose devotion is unwavering. But for how long? What if it only lasts for a year? A firmness in faith is a wonderful thing, but it is only powerful when it is combined with steadiness. Steadiness implies someone who is in for the long haul. Someone committed to always putting one foot in front of the other. To me, this is what characterizes loyal, consistent disciples. Their steadiness is the reason they are firm. —DB

Reflect and Respond

How do you demonstrate steady, consistent faith in your life?

Your favorite scripture in Helaman 6

HELAMAN 7:9

But behold, I am consigned that
these are my days.

Have you ever wanted to pick the time period when you most wanted to live? I have three—*Downton Abbey, Out of Africa,* and *17 Miracles.* Yes, I know those are all movies or TV shows, but they also represent distinct time periods, and when I watch those programs, I find myself wanting to have lived in that time. Maybe it's the clothes, or how slow life was, or the simplicity. I don't know. But those three eras call to my soul. So I can completely relate to Nephi when he says, "Oh, that I could have had my days in the days when my father Nephi first came out of the land of Jerusalem, that I could have joyed with him in the promised land; then were his people easy to be entreated, firm to keep the commandments of God, and slow to be led to do iniquity; and they were quick to hearken unto the words of the Lord" (Helaman 7:7). I think in his excitement to go back, he forgot that Lehi lost two of his sons, that a whole people broke off in anger; he might have forgotten about the broken bow and the tied-up wrists and the eating raw meat in the wilderness. "Yea, if my days could have been in those days, then would my soul have had joy. . . . But behold, I am consigned that these are my days" (Helaman 7:8–9). Isn't it interesting how easy life looks in the time period we don't currently live in? How much joy we think we might have had? But perhaps each of us has been born into the place where we are for a purpose. Just as Nephi poured out his heart on the tower in the middle of the garden and testified of the reality of the Lord, we too have a great work to do in our areas of influence. These are our days. The Lord has a work for us to do right here where we are. —EBF

Reflect and Respond
Why do you think you were saved for this time?

Your favorite scripture in Helaman 7

HELAMAN 8:7

There were some who did cry out: **Let this man alone, for he is a good man**, and those things which he saith will surely come to pass.

When Nephi stood up against the corruption of the people of his city, there was push back from those who were benefiting from the crimes he was speaking against. They started to stir people up against him—to silence him. But there were some who would not be silent. There in the city were some who cried out in his defense: "Let this man alone!"

I have a friend who was in the Marriott Center at Brigham Young University as a student when a man walked in with a device he claimed was a bomb. President Howard W. Hunter, who at that time was President of the Quorum of the Twelve Apostles, was at the pulpit speaking when the man stormed the stage and threatened his life. The man yelled threats into the microphone while President Hunter stood there calm as a summer's morning. As if it were rehearsed, the students who were in attendance for the devotional started to sing, "We Thank Thee, O God, for a Prophet." The singing, which came from all around the stand, distracted the would-be bomber just enough for security guards and students to rush the stage to tackle him to the ground. I loved hearing that students decided to rush the stage in the defense of an Apostle of the Lord. It made me wonder what I would have done.

The odds of an event happening like this again are pretty low, but the chances to defend a prophet will come often. When his messages are railed on, will we speak up, with words or with actions, to cry out, "Let this man alone, for he is a good man"? —DB

Reflect and Respond

In what ways can you defend the prophets and their words?

Your favorite scripture in Helaman 8

HELAMAN 9:39

There were some also, who believed because
of **the testimony of the five**, for they had been
converted while they were in prison.

When Nephi announced the murder of the chief judge by inspiration, five men were sent to discover if it was true. Just like with all of the people who had heard Nephi's prophecy, their hearts were filled with doubt. *We do not believe,* they said as they went, but still, they ran in their might to see. The sequence of events that followed led to them being wrongly accused, put in jail, and then brought before a judge. There they testified that what Nephi had told them was true. When the judge recognized them as the five who were sent, they were quickly released from jail, but Nephi was still not off the hook. It took another prophecy before the people believed. The verse at the end of this story teaches an important lesson: "There were some of the Nephites who believed on the words of Nephi; and there were some also, who believed because of the testimony of the five" (Helaman 9:39).

Are you one of the five? One who allows your doubt to turn to belief and then testifies to others of what you have learned?

It doesn't matter if we go through times of disbelief or if we run in our might to see if what the prophet says is true. What matters is that, once we have received a testimony that the prophet is speaking the words of God, we must share it. Because some might believe the words of the prophet, but others might believe the testimony of those who have tried out his words and experienced the truth for themselves.

I love the thought of the five who were sent, who were willing to see if the prophet spoke the truth, and, when they recognized it, testified. I want to be one of those. —EBF

Reflect and Respond

What counsel from the prophet would you like to receive a testimony of?

Your favorite
scripture in
Helaman 9

HELAMAN 10:5

Because thou hast done this with such unwearyingness, behold, I will bless thee forever.

Each night before I go to bed, I look on a few websites that scan the internet for good deals. I am addicted to good deals. Sometimes I feel like I am getting money instead of spending it. Perhaps because I love a good return on my investment, I was drawn to this teaching from Elder Neal A. Maxwell: "The usual gifts and their derivatives we give to Him could be stamped justifiably 'Return to Sender,' with a capital *S*. Even when God receives this one gift in return, the fully faithful will receive 'all that [He] hath' (D&C 84:38). What an exchange rate!" ("Consecrate Thy Performance," *Ensign*, May 2002).

In one of the greatest compliments and promises in scripture, the Lord told Nephi that He recognized that he had served Him, sought His will, and done His will with undying unwearyingness. No matter the cost, Nephi was loyal to His God. In His typical fashion of returning gold for the dust we offer, the Lord told Nephi that He would bless him forever.

Nephi's display of loyalty—for a relatively short yet significant amount of time—was returned with an eternal promise from the Almighty God, a blessing that would never end. It was an all-for-all exchange that left Nephi with an incredible return on investment. Our relationship with God is not a consumer relationship, but rather a loving covenant one. However, it must be said that when we enter into a covenant with the Lord, we come away receiving so much more than we ever have a chance to give. It is another testament to the incredible goodness of God. —DB

Reflect and Respond
What could an unwearied loyalty to God look like in your life?

Your favorite scripture in Helaman 10

HELAMAN 11:7

And it came to pass that the people saw
that they were about to perish by famine, and **they
began to remember** the Lord their God.

There are some things I am always good at. I am good at making cookies. I am good at mowing the lawn. I am good at telling stories. But there are some things I am not good at. One of those is remembering. I am terrible at remembering birthdays, and remembering deadlines, and remembering stuff at the grocery store. So it brings me great comfort in this verse that when the people saw they were about to perish by famine, they *began* to remember the Lord. Sometimes I forget. I love that in those moments it's okay to *begin* to remember.

Because I know I am bad at remembering, I have learned to set up plenty of reminders for myself. I make double alarms on my cell phone. Sometimes I wear all my rings on one finger because the uncomfortableness reminds me that I am trying to remember something, I often write things on the palm of my hand. These are tricks to help me begin to remember.

I also have spiritual reminders that help me remember the Lord. Paintings that hang on my walls. A Christ-centered playlist. Scripture verses placed throughout the house. Even the sacrament is a sacred time for helping me begin to remember.

Don't worry if you aren't good at remembering—just find things that will help you begin to remember. Those little reminders will draw your heart to Him. —EBF

Reflect and Respond

What are some things that help you begin to remember?

Your favorite
scripture in
Helaman 11

HELAMAN 12:13

Yea, and if he say unto the earth—Move—it is moved.

If I ask my children to do something, they usually don't do it. We are working on this, especially with my teenage children. I probably don't need to explain this to you.

With God, this is altogether different. When He speaks, it happens. Oh, to have that kind of authority. I love when the Psalmist said, "By the word of the Lord were the heavens made; and all the host of them by the breath of his mouth. . . . For he spake, and it was done" (Psalm 33:6, 9). He spoke and put the sun in motion, and it rises and sets each day without fail. The oceans' pull and push started at His word, and they have not stopped since creation's dawn. When God speaks, it is done.

There is something admirable about the earth in these verses. It listens and obeys every time. When I read this verse, I am tempted to make dirt my hero. What if I lived like dirt? When the Lord says to dirt, *Move*, it moves. How admirable. Perhaps I should follow dirt's pattern.

But then I quickly remember that I already have a real hero who established that pattern—Jesus. When His Father speaks, Jesus responds. Everything He does is in answer to the word of the Father. The most impressive part of it is that dirt can't say no, but Jesus can. He has the power and ability to disobey, He just doesn't. It is not in His nature. When His Father says, *Move*, He moves. He is my hero. I want to live like Him. —DB

Reflect and Respond
What word has God spoken to you? Have you moved yet?

Your favorite scripture in Helaman 12

HELAMAN 13:3

But behold, the voice of the Lord came unto him,
that he should return again, and prophesy unto the people
whatsoever things should come into his heart.

Lately I have been fascinated with the workings of the Spirit. I have learned that it has the power to guide us into places we should go, give us insight and ideas, distil upon us a sense of peace or a voice of warning, bring things back to our memory, enlarge our understanding, and prophesy unto us what we should say.

It's this last one that has become a gift in my life recently. My children have all grown up. Most of them have started their professions. The decisions they are making are huge, and life changing, and sometimes a little bit overwhelming. Lots of times they call for advice. I am not always smart in proportion to how grown up they are. I used to be able to give suggestions, insight, and help. But I don't always know how they should respond to a boss, if they should buy a home, whether they should ask for a raise. I can give advice, but I don't *know*. I have taken to praying for the Spirit many times during the midst of a conversation: *Help me know how to respond. What is the right counsel to give here? Send me an idea that might help.* Sometimes I find myself giving the oddest suggestion, only to find out days later it was exactly the right counsel for the moment at hand. In those moments I realize the counsel didn't come from me. I just spoke the words that were put into my heart. —EBF

Reflect and Respond

How have you seen the Spirit working in your life recently?

Your favorite
scripture in
Helaman 13

HELAMAN 14:11

For this intent have I come up upon the walls
of this city, that ye might hear and know...

Samuel, the Lamanite prophet, first went into the city of Zarahemla through the front doors to preach. When he was rejected and kicked out, the Lord told him to return. This time, he took a different tactic: he climbed up the outer walls to speak what the Lord put into his heart. Perhaps there were some who looked up at him and wondered, "Why did that man come back? And why in the world is he on the wall? What would possess or inspire him to do that?" Well, he told them: To give good news. "For behold, [Jesus] surely must die that salvation may come" (Helaman 14:15). For this intent—for this reason—in order to share that message, he climbed the wall and stood in a hailstorm of arrows and stones.

Perhaps that is a question that you and I will be asked throughout our lives in connection with the things we do. Why did you come to this place for eighteen months at your own expense? Why do you consistently gather your family for study of the word? Why do you keep returning to that house that gives you the cold shoulder every time? Why do you keep texting? Why do you keep serving? Why do you keep inviting? Perhaps our answer will reflect Samuel's—for this intent. For this reason: To teach of Jesus.

What if we asked the Lord those same questions? Why do you endure the whips, the spitting, the thorns? Why would you stay after the betrayal, the denial, the unfair trial? Why have you come? His answer—for this intent. For this reason: You. —DB

Reflect and Respond
What is your intent for continuing in the effort the Lord puts into your heart?

Your favorite
scripture in
Helaman 14

HELAMAN 15:6

**Yea, I say unto you, that the more part of them are
. . . striving with unwearied diligence . . .**

One week before my oldest son, Caleb, came home from his mission, he sent me a picture of his shoes with one line that said, "What do you think? Should I bring these home?"

I had never seen a pair of shoes in such bad shape. The soles were worn completely through, the stitching had come out where his toes would be, the heels were completely worn down. In that moment I realized how many miles Caleb had walked on his mission. How many stairs he had climbed. How many doors he had knocked on. In my eyes, those shoes were a representation of his unwearied diligence. "Yea, . . . they are striving with unwearied diligence that they may bring the remainder of their brethren to the knowledge of the truth; therefore there are many who do add to their numbers daily" (Helaman 15:6). Those shoes were a witness of his unwearied diligence. I wrote back and told him to bring them home.

Now those shoes sit in the office where I write. They remind me of the familiar words in Doctrine and Covenants 123:13, "Therefore, that we should waste and wear out our lives . . ." It's how I want my life to look when I am finished. In fact, the other day I told Greg what I wanted him to write on my gravestone: "Wasted and worn out." I want to live every single day of my life giving my best, with unwearied diligence, to the work of the Lord. —EBF

Reflect and Respond

Where are you serving with unwearied diligence in your life right now?

Your favorite
scripture in
Helaman 15

HELAMAN 16:15

Nevertheless, the people began to harden their hearts, all save it were **the most believing part** of them.

I can't read that last line of this phrase without wondering whether I would be included in that group or not—"the most believing part." The ones who did not harden their hearts. It reminds me of the conversation that Jesus had with Peter and the other disciples after His sermon on the bread of life. John tells us that after Jesus gave His sermon, "many of his disciples went back, and walked no more with him. Then said Jesus unto the twelve, Will ye also go away? Then Simon Peter answered him, Lord, to whom shall we go?" (John 6:66–68).

They were there to stay—the most believing part.

Not too long ago, our friends' basement suddenly flooded. I got a text from my wife about it while I was at work and couldn't get away. After it was cleaned up, I texted her to ask how everything was. She responded that it was all good, and then told me it went quickly because a lot of people came. "Oh, who came?" I asked. Her response: "The usual people." She didn't even need to tell me who it was because I already knew. The group I would call the most willing part. Or perhaps the most loyal part. You might call them the most faithful part. The book of Helaman calls them the most believing part. My hope is to be included with all of those. —DB

Reflect and Respond

Who do you know who would be included in the most believing part?

Your favorite scripture in Helaman 16

3 NEPHI 1:13

On this night shall the sign be given,
and on the morrow come I into the world.

At our house, we start counting down the days for a missionary's return at sixty-five. I don't know why we picked that number. It's just what we do. As we count down, the anticipation begins to build. That last week is excruciating. When our son Josh was about to come home this was the process we went through. It was January. There was nothing exciting to look forward to except for Josh coming home. The day before, I did all the things I always do. I got his room completely ready. I went to the grocery store and bought his favorite food. We made posters, and cleaned the house, and marked off every single hour. And then we got a phone call. He was going to be delayed twenty-four hours because of a huge storm that was coming. All of the flights were canceled. I couldn't believe it! That extra twenty-four hours about put us over the edge.

I often wonder if the people in 3 Nephi felt this same way. They had been waiting a long time for the Savior to come. They wondered when it would happen. Finally, the Lord spoke to His prophet, "Lift up your head and be of good cheer; for behold, the time is at hand, and on this night shall the sign be given, and on the morrow come I into the world" (3 Nephi 1:13).

Sometimes we watch steadfastly, we cry to the Lord throughout that day, we wait and we plan and we hope. We must remember that no matter how dark and troublesome that day may be, tomorrow will come. The 3 Nephi story is one of my favorites for this reason: sometimes we have to hold on to the truth that what we are desperately praying for today will eventually come to pass. In His own time and in His own way, He will send the answer we need *on the morrow.* —EBF

Reflect and Respond

What are some ways you have learned to watch steadfastly, cry unto the Lord, and trust?

Your favorite scripture in 3 Nephi 1

3 NEPHI 2:1

The people began to forget those signs and wonders which they had heard, **and began to be less and less astonished** at a sign or a wonder from heaven.

We live in a world of bigger and better. The phones and movie special effects and car features that were magnificent and miraculous ten years ago are considered outdated and boring today. I thought this while riding on a plane recently. I was flying in a metal tube across the country while watching a movie on the seat back in front of me and texting my friend who was on the ground. And yet, I wasn't fascinated by any of it. In fact, I was a little annoyed that the texts were taking so long to load, and there was a static line that scrolled up the LCD screen every few seconds that got so distracting I almost wanted to switch seats. Somehow, I lost the wonder of all these amazing technological feats. They had become commonplace and almost expected.

I don't know what to do about my technology snobbiness, but I hope this same non-chalance for amazing things never spills into the spiritual part of my life. I never want to lose the wonder and majesty for the things of God. I want to still have my breath taken away when I figuratively see His hand or hear His voice or witness His miracles in my life today. Instead of being less and less astonished, I hope to always be more and more grateful that God would even consider continuing to be so good to me and to this world. I hope my admiration and my astonishment just keeps getting bigger and better. —DB

Reflect and Respond

Consider the astonishing events and signs that are happening in your life right now. How could you become more grateful?

Your favorite scripture in 3 Nephi 2

_____

_____

3 NEPHI 3:5

… because of your firmness in that which ye believe to be right, and **your noble spirit in the field of battle**.

One day when my daughter Grace was walking down the busy hallway of her high school, a scuffle at the end of the hall caught her eye. There were a bunch of kids in a circle yelling profanity and ripping up the pages of a book and tossing them on the floor. As she got closer, she realized it was the Bible, and all of the pages were being crumpled by the feet of those passing by.

A boy just in front of her yelled at the boys in the circle to stop, but they didn't listen. "Why?" they yelled back. "This book isn't important to us." He quietly replied, "It's important to me." Then he bent down and started picking up the pages up off the floor and holding them tight to his chest. This made the boys in the circle mad. One of them kicked him. They shouted profanity at him. Then the boy holding the book ripped out one last section and threw the book at the boy who was helping, and they all turned and walked away.

By now Grace had walked up to where he was. "How did you have the courage to do that?" she asked as she knelt beside him and started picking up the remaining pages off the floor. "I didn't," he said. "I just knew I had to do something." And then he said something she wouldn't quickly forget: "I have been praying to know if I have enough courage to actually serve a mission. This lets me know I do. It was the answer I was praying for."

Sometimes there are heroes in our very midst who do things because of their firmness in that which they believe to be right and their noble spirit in the field of battle. —EBF

Reflect and Respond

When have you seen someone stand up for what they believed?
What did you learn from them?

Your favorite scripture in 3 Nephi 3

3 NEPHI 4:33

And their hearts were swollen with joy, **unto the gushing out of many tears**, because of the great goodness of God in delivering them out of the hands of their enemies.

I watched this horrifying security video footage on the news the other day that showed a mother desperately trying to resuscitate her choking baby. She was sitting at the mall with a few little kids when she noticed her littlest was choking on something and quickly began to perform lifesaving techniques on her child. Soon after, a police officer on duty at the mall noticed what was going on and quickly took over. Seconds and then minutes passed as the mother watched with praying hands and pacing feet her worst nightmare unfold in front of her. The diligent officer continued to administer to the little boy. Finally, in what seemed like a last-minute rescue, the baby coughed up the lodged piece of food and turned from lifeless to lively. The mother collapsed onto the baby and then melted into the arms of the police officer. She just cried and cried. Gushing out tears of gratitude, relief, and the sense of being rescued, she would not let go of her baby or pull her face off of the shoulder of the police officer. Others gathered around with tender hands on backs, applause, and more tears of praise.

How many times has this type of scene happened? How often has God orchestrated the rescue and deliverance of His children from enemies? Sometimes things do not end this way in mortality, but this will be the ending for all of our stories eventually. Sin, death, and any other enemy have been conquered, and one day we will all get our grateful, relieved, praising, tear-gushing moment with our Rescuer. —DB

Reflect and Respond

What has God done in your life that has swollen your heart with joy and filled your eyes with tears?

Your favorite scripture in 3 Nephi 4

3 NEPHI 5:14

...that the prayers of those who have gone hence,
who were the holy ones, should be fulfilled.

I have always been intrigued by the word *holy.*

The Bible Dictionary teaches that "according to the Old Testament things or places were holy that were set apart for a sacred purpose; the opposite of holy is therefore common or profane. . . . In the writings of the Prophets it is clearly laid down that the value of worship in the eyes of God depends upon the personal character of the worshipper" (Bible Dictionary, "Holiness").

The word *holiness* is synonymous with the words *consecrated* and *set apart.* When we see chiseled into the temple the phrase "Holiness to the Lord," it could also say, "consecrated to the Lord" or "set apart to the Lord." The same can be true of us. If we want to be considered *holy ones,* then our lives must be set apart and consecrated to a sacred purpose.

Brigham Young counseled, "Every moment of my life must be holiness to the Lord" (*Deseret News,* April 2, 1862, 313). Every moment of my life must be *set apart* to the Lord. Every moment of my life must be *consecrated* to the Lord. Holiness comes from consecration. I can't help but think to myself, *What would it look like to walk in holiness? To be considered one of the holy ones?* —EBF

Reflect and Respond

What does holiness look like to you? How are you seeking holiness in your life?

Your favorite scripture in 3 Nephi 5

3 NEPHI 6:20

And there began to be **men inspired from heaven**
and sent forth, standing among the people in all
the land, preaching and testifying boldly.

There was a time in high school when I felt like I was in a tailspin spiritually. I was filled with doubt, and temptation seemed to be on a full-court press. On a particularly lost day, I left English class for a few minutes to walk the halls. As I walked down one of the upstairs hallways, I heard a voice call my name from behind. It was a priest in my quorum whom I didn't know very well. I waited for him as he closed the gap between us. He walked right up to me, put his hand on my shoulder for a second, and then said, "Hey, I'm glad I found you today. I prayed I would. For some reason I have been thinking about you. I want you to know that I am here for whatever you need. Are you doing okay?" I actually lied through my teeth and told him everything was fine, but thanked him for caring so much. As we both walked away, though, I thanked my Heavenly Father for sending someone as an answer to prayer. For me, at that time, that orchestrated encounter was just enough to spark my faith.

This has always been God's pattern. In times of trouble, like the one Mormon records in 3 Nephi, whenever doubt fills the air or the earth is grappling for meaning, "men [and women] inspired from heaven" are sent forth among the people. They come as chosen prophets, leaders, neighbors, and friends. And each of them preaches hope and testifies of truth in his or her own way. —DB

Reflect and Respond

When have you witnessed men or women being inspired from heaven and sent for your benefit?

Your favorite scripture in 3 Nephi 6

3 NEPHI 7:18

It were not possible that they could disbelieve
his words, for so great was his faith on the Lord Jesus
Christ that **angels did minister unto him daily**.

Chapter 7 of 3 Nephi is filled with the work of a prophet. Preaching repentance. Raising the dead. Testifying of Christ. The church was in turmoil. The people were divided one against another. There were few righteous among them. It was a time when people did not want to listen to the prophet, and yet Nephi did not slow down. "He did minister many things unto them; and all of them cannot be written, and a part of them would not suffice, therefore they are not written in this book. And Nephi did minister with power and with great authority" (3 Nephi 7:17).

Nephi was a prophet on a mission. His focus was on the Lord and His work, and nothing was going to hold him back. It didn't matter if the people wouldn't listen, didn't believe in revelation, were angry with the direction the Lord would have him take. All that mattered was testifying boldly of Jesus Christ. He reminds me of another prophet I know. I am a little bit sad about that part in the verse that says all of the things he did could not be written, and a part of them would not suffice. Wouldn't you like to know what was taking place in the church, in the homes, in the lives of the people because of his revelation? What we do know is that it wasn't possible to disbelieve his words, because of his great faith, and that angels ministered to him daily.

He is a prophet I would have loved to meet, and it makes me even more grateful for the prophet we have today. —EBF

Reflect and Respond

What are some of your favorite prophetic quotes?

Your favorite
scripture in
3 Nephi 7

3 NEPHI 8:1

**. . . for he truly did many miracles
in the name of Jesus.**

When Jesus was on the earth, He went about doing good. He healed the sick, comforted those in mourning, and sat with those whom no one else would sit with. Today, He still does these things, but it is often through other people whom He sends in His place to heal, and to comfort, and to sit with.

A friend told me a story he witnessed in a hospital waiting room. A woman was in tears. Her daughter and son-in-law had been the cause of a terrible car accident that left them battered and being interrogated by police officers. Thankfully, tragedy with the family in the other vehicle was miraculously avoided, but the situation for the two who had been driving the car that caused the accident was not going to end well financially or legally. The mother of the guilty daughter helplessly sat in sadness and disbelief. How was her world crumbling like this? She was on the phone with her own mother when she said, "Why has the Lord abandoned this family?" My friend later learned that the mother responded on the other end by asking, "Who is there with you?" She simply replied, "The bishop." The wise mother then said, "That means that Jesus is there. He hasn't abandoned your family."

That bishop would have been uncomfortable with the way that was said, but the truth is, he was there in Jesus's name. He was there to heal and to sit and to comfort the same way Jesus would do if He had been there. —DB

Reflect and Respond
In what ways could Jesus use you to do mighty miracles in His name?

Your favorite
scripture in
3 Nephi 8

3 NEPHI 9:14

And **whosever will come, him will I receive**;
and blessed are those who come unto me.

One of my favorite New Testament stories is the story of the wedding supper found in Luke 14. A great supper was planned, and when it was ready the Lord sent his servant out to gather the people. But everyone refused to come—one was busy with his oxen, another with his wife, a third was busy with his land. So the Lord told the servant, "Bring in hither the poor, and the maimed, and the halt, and the blind." And the servant did, and still there was room. So the Lord said, "Go out into the highways and hedges, and compel them to come in, that my house may be filled" (Luke 14:21, 23; see also vv. 16–24).

I love reading about the ones the Lord invited, the unlikely, those in the margins. The poor and the blind, the ones in the highways and the hedges. *Come to my table,* He offered, *and I will fill you.* It becomes clear to me every time I read it that the people who came were the people who longed to be filled.

The invitation found in 3 Nephi 9:14–15 is a good companion scripture for this parable, "Behold, mine arm of mercy is extended towards you, and whosever will come, him will I receive; and blessed are those who come unto me. Behold, I am Jesus Christ the son of God."

When Jesus comes to the table, He looks around to see who is missing, and then He starts giving invitations. It is His way. Everyone is invited to come—everyone. He has saved a seat at the table for you. —EBF

Reflect and Respond

How have you been blessed after accepting an invitation from the Lord?

Your favorite
scripture in
3 Nephi 9

3 NEPHI 10:10

Their mourning was turned into joy,
and their lamentations into the praise and thanksgiving
unto the Lord Jesus Christ, their Redeemer.

This verse on its own is not nearly as powerful without the several chapters before it. There were storms and fires and earthquakes the land had never known before. There was darkness so thick no light could penetrate it. There was tragedy and terrible remorse of conscience. The people literally lost everything right before their eyes.

If you walked into my parents' home today, you would find lots of happiness, thanksgiving, and praise from the people who live there. The décor is as beautiful as the feeling is when you walk in the front door. It seems like an admirable little slice of heaven. If you walked in a few years ago, you would have seen sadness, questions, and mourning. After a hurricane sat unmoved over their city and a levee system collapsed, their entire house, along with their neighbors' homes, was left in wreckage and debris. When the waters receded and they walked in, everything they had was lost. Because of heaven-sent strength, their home was rebuilt and became their witness of the goodness of God and their hope in humanity. He turned their mourning into joy and "their lamentations into . . . praise and thanksgiving."

He can do this with homes, He can do this with cities, and He is particularly fond of doing this with lives. —DB

Reflect and Respond

Have you ever had or seen a moment when mourning was transformed into joy? Where did you see God's hand in it?

Your favorite scripture in 3 Nephi 10

3 NEPHI 11:14

. . . that ye may know . . .

After the earthquake and the thick darkness, Jesus came bringing peace and light. He began by introducing Himself as the one whom the prophets testified would come into the world, but He is never just about a formal introduction. The very next thing He did was to invite everyone who was there to come, one by one, and feel the prints of the nails in His hands and in His feet. "Arise and come forth," He invited, ". . . that ye may know that I am the God of Israel, and the God of the whole earth" (3 Nephi 11:14).

I have often wondered what that visit would have been like, how it would have felt to be that close to the Savior. To experience His Atonement firsthand. To know of a surety. One day, as I was thinking about that experience, I thought how the same can actually be true for each of us today. In our darkest moments, when the world is unsteady and we don't know where to turn, He invites us to come to Him, to experience the gift of His Atonement, to see and feel and come to know of a surety that He is the God of every one of us. Individually. Personally. Those experiences can happen today just as they did back then, one by one.

The scriptures do not mention how long it took; the only thing that is mentioned is that they all went forth. Every single one. No one was forgotten, or looked over, or missed. There was time for everyone. It is true. Somehow Jesus makes time for all of us, for meeting us where we are, for extending invitations, for allowing us to feel things, and for personal experiences. So that we can know. —EBF

Reflect and Respond

What are some personal experiences that have allowed you to know Jesus Christ?

Your favorite scripture in 3 Nephi 11

3 NEPHI 12:3

Blessed . . .

Through the Beatitudes—blessings and promises that have stood the test of time—the Lord showed the Nephites the way to live a happy life. Those simple statements have prompted me to write my own constitution for a blessed life:

When you feel you are lacking you are blessed
  because you will find your abundance in Him.
When your heart is broken you are blessed
  because He will come to mend you.
When you become content where you are you are blessed
  because you will learn to see God in everything.
When you are empty and unsatisfied you are blessed
  because He will come to fill you.
When you offer your heart to someone in need you are blessed
  because your heart will become like His.
When you seek for the good you are blessed
  because that is where you will find God.
When your relationships need reconciliation you are blessed
  because your Father is the giver of peace.
When you feel like you don't belong you are blessed
  because He has already welcomed you in.

In somewhat of a great reversal, the Lord taught us all that we are most blessed when we lack, when we are broken, and when we fall—for we fall right into the arms of His abundant and healing embrace. —DB

Reflect and Respond

Perhaps you would like to write your own constitution for a blessed life. Use the Savior's Beatitudes as a starting point.

Your favorite scripture in 3 Nephi 12

_____

_____

3 NEPHI 13:28-30

Consider the lilies of the field . . .

For as long as I can remember, this has been one of my favorite scriptures. It is a verse I have held on to on some of my darkest days. If He remembers a flower in a field, surely the Lord will remember me, clothe me, consider me. When Greg lost his job, when Josh was diagnosed with diabetes, when I was in bed with several hard pregnancies, I considered the lilies.

Many years ago, we had the opportunity to visit the Holy Land. On our first morning in Israel we took a long walk up the Galilean hillside. The dirt path gave way to a grassy hillside dotted with white and yellow flowers, and it was there that I discovered my first Jerusalem lily. A lily of the field, the one that scripture reminds us to consider . . . how it grows. The verse whispered through my mind as I looked at the beautiful red flowers, similar to delicate red poppies, dotting the hillside, and I remembered how *He clothes the lilies of the field.*

The lilies were there in Capernaum when we visited Peter's house, and in Magdala where Mary lived. When we visited the sites in Jerusalem, I saw them again. Bethesda. The pool of Siloam. The meadow where David faced Goliath. There again in Gethsemane. Like a fingerprint, the delicate red flowers became beautiful reminders of how the Lord will meet us in our stories. Every time I saw them, I was reminded of a God who shows up in unexpected places. A God who gives beauty, who fights battles, who sends angels, and who empowers His people to do remarkable things. A God who meets us in our need, bringing unexpected grace. —EBF

Reflect and Respond

Consider the lilies in your own life. When has the Lord shown up unexpectedly in your story, bringing a reminder of His love?

Your favorite scripture in 3 Nephi 13

3 NEPHI 14:11

If ye then, being evil, know how to give good gifts unto
your children, how much more shall **your Father who is
in heaven** give good things to them that ask him?

A chamber of my heart that I didn't even know was there opened the day my oldest
son was born. I was shocked at the way I could love. That same experience has happened
several times over for me as new little ones have joined our family. That first time we left
the hospital, my wife was being wheeled down the hallway by the nurse, and I followed
with a filled diaper bag draped over one shoulder and a new little man in tow—his car-
seat handle nestled awkwardly in the bend of my elbow.

I stopped for a moment at the administration desk to fill out the birth certificate.
Name of patient: Jack. Relationship to patient: . . . I paused before writing a new word I
never had called myself before . . . *Dad.* That's when that new heart chamber opened up.
I saw my son, I saw the world, and most particularly I saw God differently that day. He
was still the Almighty Sovereign of the universe, but on that day and in that place, I saw
Him for the first time as a Father. A Father who loved and cared in a far more divine way
than I was just beginning to—but in a way I was beginning to see more clearly.

He is not our boss or judge or dictator. He is our Heavenly Parent. And just like we
come to know how to love and care for those who are our children, how much more is
He able to "give good things to them that ask him"? —DB

Reflect and Respond

When have you seen the love of God manifested as a tender father?

Your favorite
scripture in
3 Nephi 14

3 NEPHI 15:12

Ye are my disciples; and **ye are a light** unto this people.

When the disciples gathered on the hillside in Galilee during Jesus's earthly ministry, the Master invited those hearing Him to live as "the light of the world. A city that is set on an hill cannot be hid" (Matthew 5:14).

When my wife, Jenny, was a student living at the BYU Jerusalem Center for a study abroad, the campus chose this scripture as their theme scripture for the semester. In conjunction with the theme, the Center would leave its lights on at night as a reminder of the hope Jesus had for His disciples to be a "light unto this people." Once, as Jenny and the other students were walking through the old city shopping for souvenirs and fresh-baked bread, a local merchant stopped them for conversation and ironically asked, "Are you from that little city on the hill?" "Yes," she answered. He responded, "I thought so. I can see it in your eyes."

What does it mean to be a light unto people? Interestingly, the title of "Light of the World" is a title that the Savior gave to Himself. So when He asked His disciples to take it upon them, He was asking them to live and love like He does. As His disciples, each of us can shine hope into dark places and comfort mourning souls with the same light that He has poured into our hearts. —DB

Reflect and Respond

In your circumstances and circles, how can you live as a light to the people around you? What does it look like to live and love like Jesus?

Your favorite scripture in 3 Nephi 15

3 NEPHI 16:3

They shall hear my voice, and shall be
numbered among my sheep.

When I was younger, we raised a small flock of sheep. Every small flock will generally have a lead sheep, and ours was named Big Mama. She loved my dad. When she heard him calling, she would run from the far back corner of the field to get to him. Big Mama looked like all the other lambs, but she didn't sound like them. Something wasn't quite right about her "baa," but my dad could mimic it exactly. They would talk back and forth to each other throughout the day, my dad and Big Mama.

One morning the sheep went missing. My dad figured they had gone under the fence by the irrigation ditch and into the acreage of the farmer down the street. That man raised thousands of sheep. I can remember driving to his house with my dad to ask if we could have our sheep back. "Are they marked?" he asked my dad. "No," my dad answered. "Well, I'm not just going to give you seven of my sheep if you can't even tell if they are yours." My dad quickly replied, "Oh, I will know which ones are mine; they come when they are called." The farmer looked at him incredulously and then walked out of his house with us as if to say, *this I've got to see.*

My dad stood up on the tailgate of our little white truck and began calling the sheep. He made that funny "baa" noise. *I wish you could have seen that farmer's face!* For the first bit, nothing happened. The farmer was about to ask my dad to leave. And then, from the very back of the pasture, Big Mama answered back. My dad called again, and again she answered back, and then she came running to him, with six other lambs following right behind. The farmer couldn't believe it. In fact, he helped load all seven into the back of our truck. —EBF

Reflect and Respond

What could this story teach us about hearing and recognizing the voice of the Savior when He calls?

Your favorite
scripture in
3 Nephi 16

3 NEPHI 17:9

. . . and he did heal them every one . . .

One of the most beautiful invitations in all of scripture can be found in 3 Nephi 17: "Have ye any that are sick among you? Bring them hither. Have ye any that are lame, or blind, or halt, or maimed, or leprous, or that are withered, or that are deaf, or that are afflicted in any manner? Bring them hither and I will heal them" (3 Nephi 17:7).

He called out for those who were hurting, outcast, and forgotten. He wanted them to come.

In our family there are people who are hurting. If I had been there on that day, I already know who I would have brought. I can't even begin to imagine the hope that must have filled the hearts of both the hurting and the caretakers in that moment. Healing. For some people the thought of that is incomprehensible. I wish I could have been there.

We must remember that invitation wasn't extended only at the temple in Bountiful. It is an invitation He extends to all of us. He wants to heal us; He wants to make us whole. For some people, healing comes in an instant; for others it is a process that won't be complete until the Resurrection. But we have not been forgotten, and He doesn't mean to leave us hurting. The answer to the cry from Jeremiah, "Is there no balm in Gilead; is there no physician there?" (Jeremiah 8:22) is found in 3 Nephi—"and he did heal them every one." —EBF

Reflect and Respond

Whom would you bring to Him for healing? How can you do that today?

Your favorite scripture in 3 Nephi 17

3 NEPHI 18:32

. . . continue to minister . . .

I have a good friend who is gay. Our family has walked through life with him, and we have had many deep and heartfelt conversations. Many of those conversations have been discussions about God, and church communities, and love. One afternoon he texted to say he was struggling. We talked about his life and his circumstances. I asked where he felt he was lacking. He knew immediately what it was—he missed feeling spiritual things. I asked what his spiritual practices looked like. "Do you pray? Read scripture? Do you see the hand of the Lord working in your life?" We talked about what that might look like. Then I suggested maybe he needed to find a church community. "What if they don't accept me?" he wondered out loud. I prayed they would.

After our conversation, I reflected on one of my favorite scriptures in the Book of Mormon: "Nevertheless, ye shall not cast him out from among you, but ye shall minister unto him and shall pray for him unto the Father, in my name; . . . ye shall not cast him out of your synagogues, or your places of worship, for unto such shall ye continue to minister; for ye know not but what they will return . . . and I shall heal them; and ye shall be the means" (3 Nephi 18:30–32). It is how the family of God is meant to love. We receive, and minister, and pray, and as we learn to do that well, it allows the Lord to do His work—healing hearts. These verses remind us that He will heal the hearts, but we can be the means. —EBF

Reflect and Respond

What is one thing you can do to make your place of worship more welcoming to all?

Your favorite scripture in 3 Nephi 18

3 NEPHI 19:30

And behold they did pray steadfastly, without ceasing,
unto him; **and he did smile upon them**.

We have a spot in our home at the top of our staircase that has become a sacred place for me. It is where we gather for family prayer every night. It is not big or fancy, but it is beautiful. Each night, as the kids take turns praying, I cannot help but open up my eyes. I know I really should close them in reverence, but the way they pray so sincerely, in the language of a child, as if God were right there—it forces me to open my eyes and first check to see if He might be there, and then to just watch them pray. What is even more thrilling for me is to accidentally walk in on one of them kneeling by the bedside at night in personal prayer. Those are some of my most golden moments. I usually just stand in the doorway and watch through the slightly cracked-open door.

When I read these verses from 3 Nephi, I feel like I can picture it perfectly. I don't actually know what that moment looked like, but I imagine a scene similar to the ones we have had at the top of my staircase. I take His words as advice and anticipate the same outcome. The advice: to "pray on" (3 Nephi 19:26). Without ceasing. And the anticipation is that He will smile upon us as we do. —DB

Reflect and Respond
What does it look like in your life right now to pray without ceasing?

Your favorite scripture in 3 Nephi 19

3 NEPHI 20:42

For ye shall not go out with haste nor
go by flight; for the Lord will go before you, and
the God of Israel shall be your rearward.

I have never been to battle before, but from what I've seen and heard, it seems in almost all battles, when someone is going into a dangerous situation, they usually call for backup. There are so many phrases we use that identify our back as our most vulnerable spot in defense. "Watch your back." "Stabbed in the back." "I've got your back."

Usually when you enter into a battle, you dress for protection. Scriptures give us a description of the armor of God. In a letter to the Ephesians, Paul tells the Saints to put on "the whole armour of God, that ye may be able to withstand in the evil day." In it he includes our "loins girt about with truth," the "breastplate of righteousness," "feet shod with the . . . gospel," the "shield of faith . . . to quench all the fiery darts," the "helmet of salvation," and finally "the sword of the Spirit" (Ephesians 6:13–17).

In a Sunday School lesson, we once dressed a student in a makeshift armor of God as we talked about the words from Paul. When he was all decked out, I noticed something. There was no armor on his back—the most vulnerable place. I didn't think much of it then until I came across these words from the Savior: "the God of Israel shall be your rearward." I was not only thrilled that the Lord hadn't forgotten that vulnerable spot, but particularly comforted that He has decided to personally watch over the places where we need the most protection. —DB

Reflect and Respond

How do you imagine the Lord both goes before you and also stands as your rearward?

Your favorite
scripture in
3 Nephi 20

3 NEPHI 21:25

And then shall the power
of heaven come down among them;
and I also will be in the midst.

Sometimes I think we forget how close the Savior is. We forget that the pattern of His life is to show up in people's stories, to meet them where they are. Think of the woman at the well, the man at the pool of Bethesda, and the man in the Gadarenes. He met Jairus's daughter in her bedroom, Peter in the water, and Lazarus at his tomb. Perhaps you think that only happened in the New Testament, times when He was here on the earth during His ministry. The Old Testament provides a witness that He is just as present in our stories as He was for the people in Jerusalem.

Just before the children of Israel entered the promised land, Moses gathered them all together at Mount Seir so the Lord could give Moses instructions on how they would move forward, and then he gave them an important reminder: "For the Lord thy God hath blessed thee in all the works of thy hand: he knoweth thy walking through this great wilderness: these forty years the Lord thy God hath been with thee; thou hast lacked nothing" (Deuteronomy 2:7). Consider what we learn from that verse. The Lord didn't just know about the wilderness experience; He wasn't just watching over Israel from heaven for those forty years. *He had been with them* to make sure they lacked for nothing. —EBF

Reflect and Respond

Everything we read about the Savior tells us that He wants to be in our midst to bless us. When has that been true for you?

Your favorite
scripture in
3 Nephi 21

3 NEPHI 22:7

For a small moment have I forsaken thee,
but with great mercies will I gather thee.

One of the most touching moments in the history of the Restoration for me is Joseph's prayerful plea from behind the bars of Liberty Jail. As a fourteen-year-old, I went to the place where he was unjustly and harshly imprisoned. I saw the spot where during the bitter cold months of a Missouri winter—while his loved ones and friends were being chased from their homes, leaving footprints of blood in the snow—Joseph and his brothers withered away hungry, cold, and sick in a dark dungeon. I remember wondering how much a heart could take. Now in that same place there are memorial markers with the words of Joseph's prayer and God's tender answer etched into granite.

From Joseph: "O God, where art thou?" "How long shall thy hand be stayed?" "Remember thy suffering saints." And then the heavenly response: "My son, peace be unto thy soul; thine adversity and thine afflictions shall be but a small moment; and then, if thou endure it well, God shall exalt thee on high" (D&C 121:1–8).

If ever there were times when I think God should have intervened, that would have been one of them. How could that prayer not tug on His heartstrings? I think it did. But His purposes have timing. And sometimes, those purposes include moments when we feel forsaken. If our eyes could be opened, we would see that even in the moments when we feel forsaken, He never leaves, and we know that in "great mercy" He will gather us to safety and security again. —DB

Reflect and Respond

Have you ever felt left alone or forsaken by the Lord? What evidence do you have or feel that He will gather you again?

Your favorite scripture in 3 Nephi 22

3 NEPHI 23:1

Search these things . . .

Several years ago, I received a phone call from my dad. He had lost his wedding ring and my grandfather's wedding ring in the middle of a golf course—he wasn't sure where—somewhere between the third and the fifth hole. He remembered his bag tipping over somewhere on the green. That's all. The rings were irreplaceable. My dad was devastated.

For some reason, I have had a lot of experience finding lost rings, so my dad called to see if I would come and look. I remember praying before we got to the golf course that when we got there my eyes would see nothing but the rings. I don't know why. It just seemed like a good thing to pray for. We drove a golf cart to the third hole and got out. I looked around. I am not a golfer, but I tried to imagine where I would have set my bag if I *were* a golfer, and then I walked in that direction. I noticed a patch of crabgrass that looked different from everything else and thought to myself that if I started looking there, I would know where I had been. I remember walking over to the area and then feeling a strong prompting to stop, so I did, and then I looked down at my feet. There were the rings. Right there. Both of them, lying right on top of the crabgrass. I yelled out to my dad that I had found them, and he couldn't believe it. We had been on the golf course for less than ten minutes.

Some miracles come from searching, from praying that our eyes will see what we need to see. It is true with lost rings, but it is also true of scripture verses. When we search diligently, great blessings come. —EBF

Reflect and Respond

What is one way you could search diligently in your scriptures today?

Your favorite scripture in 3 Nephi 23

3 NEPHI 24:3

And **he shall sit as a refiner and purifier** of silver; and he shall
purify the sons of Levi, and purge them as gold and silver, that
they may offer unto the Lord an offering in righteousness.

Words like *refine*, *purify*, and *purge* are terms that a silversmith is familiar with. The process of producing silver and gold in the royal state—cleansed of all impurity and molded to perfection—requires an intense heating and cooling process. As a self-titled refiner, the Lord is teaching that He desires to enact a similar process of purification and purging upon us.

It reminds me of an analogy from C. S. Lewis in which God takes us from where we are and builds us into something beautiful. "At first, perhaps, you can understand what He is doing. He is getting the drains right and stopping the leaks in the roof and so on: you knew that those jobs needed doing and so you are not surprised. But presently He starts knocking the house about in a way that hurts abominably and does not seem to make any sense. What on earth is He up to? The explanation is that He is building quite a different house from the one you thought of—throwing out a new wing here, putting on an extra floor there, running up towers, making courtyards. You thought you were going to be made into a decent little cottage: but He is building a palace" (*Mere Christianity* [Touchstone: 1996], 176).

Either way, we offer ourselves as an offering to the Lord. He will refine us and build us into something only He can envision. The process to that end will be a journey indeed, but the outcome will be precious in His sight. —DB

Reflect and Respond
Where have you seen God as a refiner in your life story?

Your favorite
scripture in
3 Nephi 24

_____

_____

3 NEPHI 25:2

But unto you that fear my name, shall the Son of Righteousness arise **with healing in his wings**.

When spring comes, it brings new life. Tulips grow out of deep, black earth. Hyacinths bloom. The trees, which have been barren all winter, don't just turn green— blossoms cover the branches, filling the air with sweetness. The earth is healed in spring- time, and everything begins again.

This chapter, which talks about the Son of Righteousness who will arise with healing in his wings, is repeated from Malachi 4, and we wonder what it means. Nephi gives us clarity: "Behold, they will crucify him; and after he is laid in a sepulchre for the space of three days he shall rise from the dead, *with healing in his wings;* and all those who shall believe on his name shall be saved in the kingdom of God" (2 Nephi 25:13; emphasis added).

For those who have only Malachi's words, this verse can be confusing, especially because in the book of Malachi it reads, "Sun of Righteousness." Here the Book of Mormon brings clarification that helps us understand. The Son of man wouldn't just arise, He would rise from the dead three days after He was crucified. The healing would come through the promise of the Resurrection. From death to life. From barren to blos- som. It is the promise of the Savior, and we are reminded of it every spring: the Son of Righteousness shall arise with healing in his wings. —EBF

Reflect and Respond
Why does the Resurrection of Jesus Christ bring you hope?

Your favorite scripture in 3 Nephi 25

3 NEPHI 26:6

And now there cannot be written in this
book even **a hundredth part of the things which
Jesus did truly teach** unto the people.

A single story about the goodness of Jesus can win me over and melt my heart in loyalty to Him. Think about the leper He healed. This was a man who was considered an outcast in his society. Once he contracted the disease, he would have been sent to the place where he and the other lepers would live together in misery—their bodies aching in pain, their hearts aching more deeply in loneliness. Because of the law, this man was likely avoided like the plague. No one could touch him or come near. It had probably been a long time since anyone gave him a handshake, hug, or goodnight kiss on the cheek. His life was falling apart. Until Jesus. When Jesus came, the man ran to Him and fell down at His feet, begging Him for relief. After a brief, divine exchange, the Savior reached out and touched the man to heal him. Of all the ways He could have chosen to heal him, Jesus chose to touch the untouchable man (see Mark 1:40–42).

This experience was repeated at different times with different details, yet the same tenderness marked Jesus's ministry on both sides of the world. The things He did and the words He taught were of this caliber every time. Mormon told us that not even a hundredth of the things that He taught through word and deed were written in the book. The more I learn about Jesus, the more I want to hear those stories and learn those teachings. I long for them. I long for Him. —DB

Reflect and Respond

Which of Jesus's teachings are the most meaningful to you in your life right now?

Your favorite
scripture in
3 Nephi 26

_____

_____

3 NEPHI 27:13

This is the gospel which I have given unto you . . .

I love how Jesus explains His gospel to us. It is simply this: "I came into the world to do the will of my Father, because my Father sent me" (3 Nephi 27:13). It's that simple. I came. To do my Father's will. Because my Father sent me. And why did the Father send Him? "That I might be lifted up upon the cross; and after that I had been lifted up upon the cross, that I might draw all men unto me, that as I have been lifted up by men even so should men be lifted up by the Father" (3 Nephi 27:14).

The gospel of Jesus Christ is all about lifting. It is a message we are reminded of over and over again in scripture, "Wherefore, be faithful; stand in the office which I have appointed unto you; succor the weak, lift up the hands which hang down, and strengthen the feeble knees" (D&C 81:5).

I can't help but wonder, how am I doing at living the gospel? I look to His example. He came. To do His Father's will. Because His Father sent Him. Maybe that is how my mornings should begin, by asking those three questions: Where should I go today? What is His will for me today? What is He sending me to do today? Most important, how can I lift and draw others to Him?

What if those questions were at the top of our to-do lists? What if that mentality governed our decisions? What would the gospel look like if we approached every day like that? —EBF

Reflect and Respond

Spend some time answering the questions above. How might those answers help you to live His gospel more fully?

Your favorite scripture in 3 Nephi 27

3 NEPHI 28:1

And it came to pass when Jesus had said these words,
he spake unto his disciples, one by one, saying unto
them: **What is it that ye desire of me**...?

It has been a long time since I have made a Christmas wish list. As a kid, I loved doing that. All of the catalogs and magazines filled with pictures of toys would come in the mail in November and December, and my siblings and I would sit around the kitchen table looking through them page by page and handpicking what we hoped for and wanted most for Christmas. For most kids, Christmas and birthdays seem like the only chance you have during the year to get a gift. With no job or source of income, the more unobtainable a gift is, the better it is, and for a kid, most everything feels unobtainable. Perhaps this is why adults sometimes lose the magic of Christmas. Everything is obtainable. They can just go buy it.

But what if someone were offering you something you couldn't buy on your own? What if that someone were Jesus, and, just like He did with His disciples, what if He came to you, one-on-one, and asked you the question, "What is it that ye desire?" *What do you want or need from me?* Ask and it shall be given. I believe this *is* a question He would and does ask each of us if we are listening. What do you desire? What is your heart yearning for? It reminds me of one of His best titles, The Giver of Every Good Gift. —DB

Reflect and Respond

If Christ came to you one on-one-and asked that question—What desirest thou?—what would you say?

Your favorite scripture in 3 Nephi 28

_____

_____

3 NEPHI 29:1

. . . when the Lord shall see fit, in his wisdom . . .

Not yet. It's the answer to so many questions. Is dinner ready? Are we there? Is Dad home? It means something is about to happen, it just hasn't happened yet. Usually that something is good.

For many years the words in this book of scripture were hidden up in the ground under a hill in Palmyra. Goodness was waiting. The world wasn't ready yet. But the Lord knew when it would be time. He said, "It shall come in a day when it shall be said that miracles are done away; . . . when the power of God shall be denied, and churches become defiled and be lifted up in the pride of their hearts. . . . Yea, it shall come in a day when there shall be . . . murders, and robbing, and lying, and deceivings, and whoredoms, and all manner of abominations" (Mormon 8:26–31).

Now the book is here. This is our day, and if the Lord were here He would tell us this: "Yea, wo unto him that shall deny the revelations of the Lord, and that shall say the Lord no longer worketh by revelation, or by prophecy, or by gifts, . . . or by the power of the Holy Ghost!" (3 Nephi 29:6). From under that hill in Palmyra, New York, goodness came, because the Lord saw fit in His wisdom to send His words to a people who were surrounded by all manner of abominations. He knew the words of the book would help. But He also knew there would be some who would turn away from the book, who wouldn't believe in miracles, or revelation, or prophecy. He saw fit to send it anyway. Will we see fit to use it? —EBF

Reflect and Respond

Why do you think the Lord saw fit in His wisdom to send the Book of Mormon in our day?

Your favorite scripture in 3 Nephi 29

3 NEPHI 30:1-2

Hearken...

The Savior's ministry among the Nephites is one of the crown-jewel sections of the entire Book of Mormon. Interestingly, I just recently discovered that the time Jesus spent among them both begins and ends with a similar invitation. The first one came from the Father—"Behold my Beloved Son, in whom I am well pleased, in whom I have glorified my name—hear ye him" (3 Nephi 11:7). Just like the invitation to Joseph in the Sacred Grove, the Nephites surrounding the temple in Bountiful were invited *to hear Him.* It is instructive and intriguing to me to learn and look for what the opening truth or invitation is in any sermon—especially a sermon from Jesus. Why did the Father begin with that invitation? What do you think the Father hoped they would hear?

Just as instructive as a deliberate opening invitation, there is also great value in identifying what His parting advice and invitation was. For the Lord, it was the same as the first: "Hearken." Listen—with a willing and attentive mind and heart. In what was recorded as a short section of parting words, He taught some simple, sometimes one-word, invitations to any who heard or would later read about the time He spent among the Nephites. Consider finding and marking all the simple invitations from the Lord—perhaps the invitations He and the Father hope we will hear and hearken to.

Hearken. Hear. Turn. Repent. Come. Receive. Be filled. Be numbered. —DB

Reflect and Respond

Which of these invitations speaks to your soul right now? Why is that?

Your favorite scripture in 3 Nephi 30

4 NEPHI 1:18

How blessed were they!
For the Lord did bless them in all their doings.

When I first met David Butler, it was to plan a walk from the Draper Utah Temple to the Salt Lake Temple. The first item of business was to pick a date. I brought the paper calendar from off the back of my pantry door—that's how many years ago it was. We wanted to do a Sunday fireside to kick off the walk, so we searched through the calendar to find the best date. The date we chose already had one word written there, "blessings." "What is this?" David asked. "Is it important?" For the life of me, I couldn't remember what it was. But it was written in pen, so I figured it had to be important. "I don't know," I told him, "let me think." He looked at me funny and then said, "I think you scheduled your own blessings on the calendar." It was the most preposterous thing I had ever heard. "I don't do that," I told him, shaking my head. For the rest of our meeting I tried to remember what that word meant, but I never did. When I left, he told me, "I seriously think you schedule your own blessings." It was a couple of days later when I remembered what the word meant. My sister had adopted two babies from Tonga, and their baby blessings were on that Sunday. *"Blessings."* It made complete sense. When I called to tell David, he was a bit disappointed and said, "It was more fun when you scheduled your own blessings." So, just for fun, I bought him a brand-new calendar and scheduled blessings for him all the way through that year. That made him feel happier.

Here's something I believe about the Lord—I think He schedules blessings for us. I love the exclamation mark in the middle of this verse. I believe sending blessings is probably His favorite work. —EBF

Reflect and Respond
Has the Lord sent you a blessing recently? What was it?

Your favorite scripture in 4 Nephi 1

MORMON 1:17

But I did remain.

It must have been hard to be Mormon. He lived in a discouraging time, a time when wickedness prevailed upon the land, and the disciples were taken away. There were no miracles, no healing, and no gifts from the Lord. Even the Holy Ghost was absent because of the wickedness and unbelief (Mormon 1:13–14, 16).

Mormon was fifteen years old. For a time he tried to preach to the people, but eventually he was forbidden, and yet, he had to remain. He must have been lonely. Although he was visited of the Lord and knew of the goodness of Jesus, you can't help but wonder what he did during his waking hours. We get a small glimpse in the last verse of this chapter. Mormon tells us "there were sorceries, and witchcrafts, and magics; and the power of the evil one was wrought upon all the face of the land . . ." and then he writes something interesting, "even unto the fulfilling of all the words of Abinadi, and also Samuel the Lamanite" (Mormon 1:19). How would he have known the prophecies of Abinadi and Samuel, two men who had lived years before? He must have been reading their words . . . perhaps that was how he was spending his days. But there is something of even greater interest to me. Consider those two men—Abinadi and Samuel. Two other men who stood alone in a wicked time. Mormon's companions during those dark days were two scripture heroes who had lived through something similar. I wonder if he spent his days searching the scriptures looking for advice and counsel from someone who would understand.

We can do the same. In the discouraging times of our lives, times when we are searching for answers or direction, we can turn to the scriptures. We can search for similar stories. We can learn from the people who went before. —EBF

....

Reflect and Respond

What is going on in your life right now? Can you think of a similar situation in the scriptures? What can you learn from that example?

Your favorite scripture in Mormon 1

MORMON 2:7

And it came to pass that we did gather in our people **as fast as it were possible**.

One summer, our family was playing a baseball game at the fields that were near our house. When we started, there were blue skies and warm sunshine and fluffy white clouds dotting the sky. It was a perfect day for a ball game. While we were playing, our attention was drawn entirely to the field; no one noticed a massive storm cloud blowing in until we heard what sounded like a hundred people pounding their feet on the metal roof of a nearby building. Immediately everyone recognized it as hail and saw the cloud moving quickly toward us. As fast as we could, we grabbed the gloves, bats, and balls in the field and ran for the dugout for protection just in the nick of time. Had we not run immediately for the covering when we heard the hailstones, we would have been caught right in the middle of the deluge—it just came too quickly.

I think about this time of wickedness that the Nephites were experiencing and can see some parallels. When the call for safety came, the Nephites gathered in their people "as fast as it were possible." I wonder if I respond with that same speed to the counsel and direction of the Spirit, prophets, or other inspired Church leaders. Do I run with the same quickness as I did when I saw the hail? And if not, why not? The speed on the baseball field protected us from hail and rain. The speed in the Nephite era protected them from destruction. —DB

Reflect and Respond

What is the value to us and our families when we respond to promptings quickly?

Your favorite scripture in Mormon 2

MORMON 3:12

Behold, I had led them . . .
and had loved them . . .

My Grandpa Mickey was a coach at East High School. He coached every sport—football, baseball, track, and even swimming—because that was what a coach did in those days. He was a really good coach and he loved coaching, but he loved the boys he coached more. My grandmother kept a book at the house for visitors to sign, and more often than not the signatures were those of the boys he coached.

One year his swim team took State. It was a remarkable victory, and unexpected. The boys were so excited that they picked my grandpa up off his feet and threw him in the deep end of the pool. What no one knew, because he had never said anything, was that my grandpa had no idea how to swim. None. He had never swum a stroke in his life. So he started to drown. He really did! The boys had to jump into the deep end of that pool and save him.

Afterward they asked him how he knew how to coach a team to a state championship in a sport he had never tried. I don't know what his answer was, but I do know this: he loved those boys, and because he loved them, he led them. It didn't matter what they were trying to accomplish, he was going to give his very best effort to help them succeed. It is the mark of a good leader. If you want to lead well, love well. —EBF

Reflect and Respond
Think of one of the best leaders you know. What can you learn from that leader's example?

Your favorite scripture in Mormon 3

MORMON 4:4

And it was **because the armies of the Nephites went up unto the Lamanites** that they began to be smitten; for were it not for that, the Lamanites could have had no power over them.

I once heard some valuable advice from a man cautioning about reading certain types of books or articles. In the conversation, he talked specifically about writings that are overly critical and demeaning to Church doctrines, policies, and leadership—articles written with the intention of undermining someone's faith. While giving us a fair warning and caution about material like that, he said, "Mud never gets 'glovey' when you play in it." Here was the principle: If you are wearing gloves and playing in the mud, the gloves will always get muddy, but mud never gets "glovey." It is easier for the mud to impact and stain the gloves than it is for gloves to impact or change the mud.

This is true for media and entertainment but also for the people we choose to align ourselves with. (I chose the word *align* on purpose, by the way, because I believe we should always be friendly and overly kind to everyone no matter what their life choices are. Being friendly is different from *aligning* yourself with someone.)

In this time in Nephite history, the Lamanites could hurt the Nephites only if the Nephites went up unto them. If they stayed back, the Lamanites had no power. It is a good lesson for all of us. We have to live in the world surrounded by evil influences, but we don't have to go to their places of stronghold. We don't have to get muddy. —DB

Reflect and Respond

Are there places or activities or media you consume that put you in the muddy places?

Your favorite scripture in Mormon 4

MORMON 5:10

**...that realize and know
from whence their blessings come.**

One of the Nephites' greatest problems was that they were looking for Mormon to deliver them, rather than looking to the Lord. It is a mistake many of us make. We trust what we can see, our own strength or the strength of someone else, before trusting in the Lord.

I remember a particularly hard time in my life. I had a sister-in-law who was struggling, a friend whose life was in serious trouble, and a nephew whose world had been turned upside down. As a problem solver by nature, I wanted to step in and fix everything that was going wrong. I wanted to save them from each situation, but I couldn't. The problems were too big. I remember going to the temple one morning with all of their burdens weighing heavy on my heart. I went looking for advice, hoping there was something I could do to help. The temple was busy, and I spent a lot of time waiting. While I was there, I opened up the scriptures, hoping to pass the time by reading. The first few verses of the chapter I turned to jumped right out at me: "Hear, O ye heavens, and give ear, O earth, and rejoice ye inhabitants thereof, *for the Lord is God, and beside him there is no Savior. Great is his wisdom, marvelous are his ways, and the extent of his doings none can find out. His purposes fail not, neither are there any who can stay his hand*" (D&C 76:1–3). Immediately the thought came to my mind, *my job is not to save them from these situations— that is the Savior's job. His wisdom is great. His purposes fail not. No one can stay His hand. He will know what to do. My job is simply to lead these people to Him.*

Sometimes we just need a reminder of where to turn our focus, where to look for help, where our blessings will come from. When we want to remember where our greatest blessings come from, we must look to Him. —EBF

Reflect and Respond

What is one way that you have come to realize and know the blessings that come from Christ?

Your favorite
scripture in
Mormon 5

MORMON 6:17

O ye fair ones, how could ye have rejected that Jesus,
who stood with open arms to receive you!

Sometimes when my kids are playing "the floor is lava" and they spend the evening jumping from couch to couch, I warn them that someone or all of them are going to get hurt. I am all for invented games and kid adventures, but as the dad with a little more experience, I can usually sense or see what is about to go wrong. Kids are just sometimes oblivious. Without fail, I am right: disaster large or small strikes, and the game usually ends in a Band-Aid or stitches—we've had both.

I can understand how they avoid the first warning I give them—they are in the middle of having fun. What would be strange would be if they refused to come to me after they got hurt. They always do come, but whenever I read this line from Mormon, I try to think what it would be like to be willing to help my children and then to have them respond by turning their backs—to stand there with open arms and have them reject the invitation. It would seem unnatural, and it would break my fatherly heart. I cannot imagine how the Savior feels—after all that He did and all that He does in order to heal us, and at no cost to us, and for it to be denied. Heartbreaking.

After expressing this sadness, Mormon also tells those who rejected Jesus that he too mourns their loss. There is no "I told you so" or uncompassionate nonchalance—just a pleading and then a mourning from a man with a heart like Jesus. —DB

Reflect and Respond

Have you been in this place before? What do you think makes some reject the open arms of Jesus?

Your favorite scripture in Mormon 6

MORMON 7:9

If ye believe that ye will believe this also . . .

Just before my grandmother died, I asked what she had learned. She was ninety-three years old. She said there were three pieces of advice she would give me for living a happy life. First, be spontaneous. If someone ever extended an invitation, say yes! Second, express gratitude. Write thank-you cards. Make sure people know that you are grateful for them. Third, find one thing that brings happiness every single day. Those were the things that she knew, that governed her life. I love her more for this advice.

At the end of Mormon's life, he also makes a list of things he knows. It is a list of seven things, mostly contained in chapter seven, but the first two come from chapter five.

1. Know ye not that ye are in the hands of God? (5:23)
2. Know ye not that he hath all power? (5:23)
3. Know ye that ye are of the house of Israel. (7:2)
4. Know ye that ye must come unto repentance. (7:3)
5. Know ye that ye must lay down your weapons of war. (7:4)
6. Know ye that ye must come to the knowledge of your fathers. (7:5)
7. Know ye that ye must . . . believe in Jesus Christ. (7:5)

It was a list of things he knew. It's what governed his life. It is the advice he left for us as parting advice in the Book of Mormon. What do you learn from his words? —EBF

Reflect and Respond

Have you ever asked someone who is older and wiser than you for advice? What did you learn?

Your favorite scripture in Mormon 7

MORMON 8:12

Whoso receiveth this record, and shall not condemn it because of the imperfections which are in it, **the same shall know of greater things than these**.

The first time I read the Book of Mormon, I did not fully believe those words by Moroni. Yes, I know he spent a lot of time in those records, but I just wasn't seeing what he was seeing. Where were these greater things? What were they? But then I came across this quote from Elder Neal A. Maxwell, who had spent much more time in that book than I had: "I need and want additional time. For me, towers, courtyards, and wings await inspection. My tour of it has never been completed. Some rooms I have yet to enter, and there are more flaming fireplaces waiting to warm me. . . . There are also sumptuous banquet tables painstakingly prepared by predecessors which await all of us. Yet, we as Church members sometimes behave like hurried tourists, scarcely venturing beyond the entry hall to the mansion" ("The Book of Mormon: A Great Answer to 'The Great Question,'" Address at Book of Mormon Symposium, BYU, October 10, 1986).

When I read that I wondered—how does a senior member of Church leadership still feel like he has "rooms" in the Book of Mormon that he has "yet to enter"? That renewed my dedication and search for truth in the pages of the Book of Mormon. A book that, since then, has never disappointed. I can now comfortably witness that the Book of Mormon is filled with these "greater things." —DB

Reflect and Respond

What are some of the great things you have discovered in your recent study of the gospel and particularly the Book of Mormon?

Your favorite scripture in Mormon 8

MORMON 9:11

**But behold, I will show unto
you a God of miracles.**

Once, when I was reading the accounts of the last week of the Savior's life, one verse stood out to me. It was the verse in Luke 23:22, when Pilate asked the crowd, "What evil hath he done?" As I read, I wondered what would have happened if Pilate had called up witnesses in that moment to discover the works that Jesus had done—the people who had actually experienced the work of Jesus during His three-year ministry. Instead of a line of people listing the evil He had done, I imagined a line forming in the room, and these are the people I envisioned standing there:

The woman who touched His robe
The daughter of Jairus
The man who was blind from birth
The man from the pool of Bethesda
The man from the Gadarenes
The tenth leper
The man lowered down through the roof by his four friends
The centurion's servant
The boy with the demons
Lazarus
Malchus, the soldier who lost his ear

Can you imagine all of them standing there waiting to share? Consider what their witness would have been like. The first person in line could have begun with just one simple introduction, "Behold, I will show unto you a God of miracles" (Mormon 9:11). —EBF

Reflect and Respond

What are some of your favorite miracles of Christ?

Your favorite
scripture in
Mormon 9

_____

_____

ETHER 1:42-43

And there I will meet thee, and I will
go before thee . . . and there will I bless thee.

Have you ever had to do something hard? Something you didn't want to go through? Do you remember how it felt? Sometimes the Lord meets us in those places; other times He sends others to minister to us there.

In our ward, five tiny babies were born and died within the same few years. Our ward members spent those years praying for miracles, and bearing burdens, and giving comfort. When the first baby died, the Relief Society sisters decided to make a small quilt for the mother. In the center we stitched the name of the baby, and in the squares all around each woman in the ward chose one word to represent the hope and joy that baby brought. The squares included words such as *strength, angel, hope, eternity, families are forever,* and *love.* The blanket was beautiful.

Those blankets became a tradition in our ward. We made one for every baby we lost. It endeared us to each other.

I will never forget dropping off the last quilt. The thought of it still brings tears to my eyes. We walked into the living room and sat next to the mother, who looked at the blanket and whispered, "I never wanted one of these." And then she opened it up to look at the words and gathered it close in her arms and said through tears, "I love it." It was a place she didn't want to go, a road she didn't want to travel, but she knew she didn't travel it alone. Besides the eighty sisters who had stitched squares on that blanket, there were four particular squares that had been hand stitched by four other mothers who knew exactly what she was going through. I can't help but think it was the Lord's way of meeting each of those women where they were. —EBF

Reflect and Respond

Where has the Lord met you recently and how has He blessed you there?

Your favorite
scripture in
Ether 1

ETHER 2:25

Ye cannot cross this great deep **save I prepare you**
against the waves of the sea, and the winds which have
gone forth, and the floods which shall come.

The brother of Jared took three problems to the Lord concerning the barges his people would travel in to the promised land. One of them was how he was going to steer. In answer to this problem, the Lord didn't answer. The people would simply have to get into the barges and trust that the Lord would take them across the sea. I wonder what kind of personality the brother of Jared had. Did he like to be in control? Was he more comfortable if he could have his hands on a steering wheel? What was it like to get into a sailless, rudderless, motorless vessel and commend yourself to the Lord?

I can just imagine myself saying, as I stepped down into a boat I couldn't steer, *Okay, Lord, it's in your hands.* The words of comfort in this verse would have been a great strength to me as I crossed blindly. The Lord knew the waves would come, the winds would come, and the floods would come, and He had already prepared for those before the brother of Jared ever even pushed the vessel into the water. It gives me courage to step into a new adventure and change in my own life. I hear the Lord whispering a similar reassurance. *I will get you across these deep waters. I have already prepared you for what is to come.* Perhaps when a flood, wind, or wave approaches I can remind myself—it is okay, God has already strengthened me to carry this and prepared the way through it, and He will provide an escape. —DB

Reflect and Respond
Has there been a time in your life when you were prepared beforehand? What did you learn from that experience?

Your favorite scripture in Ether 2

ETHER 3:11

Believest thou the words which I shall speak?

Every time I read this question from the Lord to the brother of Jared, my immediate reaction is to ask back, "Well, what are you going to say? How do I know if I believe you if I haven't even heard it yet?" This is the way the world works: Prove it and then I will believe. From the outside working in. President Ezra Taft Benson once taught: "The Lord works from the inside out. . . . The world would take people out of the slums. Christ takes the slums out of people. . . . The world would mold men by changing their environment. Christ changes men, who then change their environment. The world would shape human behavior, but Christ can change human nature" ("Born of God," *Ensign*, November 1985).

To choose to believe is a position of trust. Belief opens the heart and invites the Lord in. Believing drops our guard and defenses and puts us in a vulnerable, intimate readiness of soul. When the brother of Jared affirms to the Lord that he will believe what he has not yet heard, it shows that he understands something about the Lord's character and nature. He knows that the Lord is for him—that all of His words, motives, intentions, prescriptions, and commands are all for his good. The same is true for each of us. When the Lord asks us if we believe something that hasn't happened, He is asking us if we trust Him with our futures. Do you and I assume and believe that He truly is and will always be the "high priest of good things to come" (Hebrews 9:11)? —DB

Reflect and Respond

What do you already believe the Lord is capable of doing with your future?

Your favorite scripture in Ether 3

ETHER 4:12

**And whatsoever thing persuadeth
men to do good is of me.**

From the very beginning pages of the Book of Mormon, we learn that communication between God and man is not just a prophet's privilege. The Lord spoke to and answered the prayers of teenagers, mothers, hunters, and missionaries—people of every kind. The dilemma that comes with a truth like this is the age-old question: How do I know if those were my own thoughts or God speaking to me? God definitely speaks, but because He often communicates through thoughts and feelings, it can be confusing. I once heard a man share a story about a thought or impression he had while serving as a young missionary. It was to give a visiting General Authority some money before he boarded a train. For years he said he wondered whether it was just his thoughts or whether that was an impression from the Lord. He never found out.

Scattered throughout the Book of Mormon are bits of wisdom that help answer this question. They are so simple, but so helpful. If it is good or persuades you to do good, it is from God. All good comes from Him.

So, was giving the money a good thought? Sure. We don't know why. It's always nice to have some extra cash on hand, just in case, and if he didn't need it, he could always buy an ice cream. All glory goes to God, no matter what the outcome. We never have to worry about who gets credit because the good thoughts that come into our minds are always inspired by and because of Him. Let this be your rule: if it is good, move on it. —DB

Reflect and Respond

Act on a good thought without wondering if it came from God or yourself. What did you discover?

Your favorite scripture in Ether 4

ETHER 5:2

. . . those who shall assist . . .

One of my favorite verses in the Doctrine and Covenants is a revelation written to a man by the name of David Whitmer. It says, "And behold, thou art David, and thou art called to assist" (D&C 14:11). I wonder what he thought about his calling.

Did you know that same David was mentioned in the Book of Mormon as well? Interestingly, he is recognized for the same gift: "And behold, ye may be privileged that ye may show the plates unto *those who shall assist* to bring forth this work; and unto three shall they be shown by the power of God; wherefore they shall know of a surety that these things are true" (Ether 5:2–3; emphasis added).

Thousands of years before it happened, Moroni wrote about a man who would be called to assist and would then have the privilege of seeing the plates. It was a job designated for David Whitmer long before he was even born. I wonder, when David heard that revelation in June of 1829, how he felt about his call to assist. How much more important did that call become when he read the prophecy about that same call to assist in a verse that had been chiseled onto plates almost 1400 years before?

We may wonder if our call is important. We may consider our assignment an afterthought. We might question the magnitude of being called to assist.

Remember, some people's entire career is built on their ability to assist, and many games have been won because of the assist that led to the final score. We must never underestimate the importance of being called to assist. —EBF

Reflect and Respond

When have you been called to assist? What did you learn from that assignment?

Your favorite scripture in Ether 5

ETHER 6:8

And it came to pass that **the wind did never cease** to blow towards the promised land while they were upon the waters.

I came home one day from the gym with a tiring realization. I said to my wife, "Exercise is never going to be easy, is it?" Her simple answer back was, "Nope." She is an exercise science major and was a personal trainer, but it does not take a degree to verify that truth. By nature, exercise is always supposed to push you beyond comfortable limits. It is designed to make you better at something—more flexible, stronger, faster. But being pushed is uncomfortable. I don't want to be stretched or to struggle. But this is the only way to the changes and benefits I am hoping to have.

When the crew at the beginning of the book of Ether put their boats into the water, we learn from their journey that the wind never did cease to blow. In case you were wondering, I believe that wind is probably the worst weather system. I wonder if they got tired of being pushed. What if they just wanted to float or coast for a minute? They could have, but then they would never have reached their promised land. The only way to cross the ocean was to be pushed across. It was the only way to the benefits and goals God had in store for them. And in the end, it was all worth it. —DB

Reflect and Respond

When have you experienced God's winds pushing you forward? As you look back, can you see where they have brought you?

Your favorite scripture in Ether 6

ETHER 7:27

And he remembered the great things
that the Lord had done for his fathers.

My mother was in a grocery store shopping when she felt a prompting to go home. It was years before cell phones or even pagers would be invented. She tried to think what she might need to be doing at home, but nothing came to mind, so she continued to shop. Again, the prompting came, and she thought it through and then continued to fill her cart. When the prompting came the third time, she left her groceries in the cart, lifted my youngest sister out, and drove home.

When she walked through the front door, the phone was ringing. It was the paramedics calling to say that my little brother had been hit by a school bus while walking home from school. They gave her the address and told her to come. She made it there in time to ride in the ambulance with my brother to the hospital. What if she hadn't gone home?

We heard that story over and over growing up. Sometimes my mom will refer to it even now, the prompting of the Spirit, the ministering of angels, the miracles. Every time I hear it, what I remember is that I have a mother who understood the importance of listening and responding to the Spirit. As I was growing up, I determined that was the kind of mother I wanted to be. —EBF

Reflect and Respond

Can you think of a great thing the Lord has done for your parents? What do you learn from their experience?

Your favorite scripture in Ether 7

ETHER 8:23

It is wisdom in God that **these things should be shown unto you**, that thereby ye may repent of your sins, and suffer not that these murderous combinations shall get above you.

I had the best history teacher in high school: Coach Madden. If you are reading this and are a history teacher, I am sorry, but you are competing for second-best history teacher. The gold medal has already been given. I never missed his class. His lessons were interesting, insightful, and interactive. It is one of the only classes I can remember from all my years growing up. During one of our classes, he took us to an auditorium where the walls had been lined with words written in a tiny font. We later learned that they all represented victims of the Holocaust. We sat in the auditorium for fifty minutes and heard the stories and watched videos and shared in a way that has remained meaningful to me after all this time. At the end of all of his lessons, he would always tell us that the reason we learn history is to make sure we never repeat the mistakes from the past. On that particular day he put exclamation points on that advice for us.

I think Coach Madden and Moroni would have gotten along. Some of the sad things and evil things that Moroni included in the Book of Mormon record were for this same purpose and to this same end. He gave the same advice to future readers that my history teacher gave to me—suffer not—do not allow these types of things to creep in. Do not let them "get above you." —DB

Reflect and Respond

What negative examples have helped you in your decision making to avoid tragedy and trouble?

Your favorite scripture in Ether 8

_____

_____

ETHER 9:35

And the people began to revive again . . .

I am so intrigued by this verse. It comes after a period of wickedness, after a time when the people believed not the words of the prophets, so the Lord sent a famine in the land. When the people thought they would perish, they began to repent of their iniquities and cried unto the Lord for help. "And it came to pass that when they had humbled themselves sufficiently before the Lord he did send rain upon the face of the earth; *and the people began to revive again,* and there began to be fruit in the north countries, and in all the countries round about. And the Lord did show forth his power unto them in preserving them from famine" (Ether 9:35; emphasis added). Perhaps because the scripture talks about the rain the Lord sent, I expected that line to say, "And the *earth* began to revive again." I am fascinated that it was the people who were revived.

Think about this—in a famine the land becomes parched and dry, what used to be full of life shrivels up and withers away, there is no life-giving source of water. Perhaps the same was true for these people. Consider what a spiritual drought might look like. It would leave you feeling empty, shriveled up, weary, and withered. Without living water, there is no life-giving source of strength. I love that when the people repented, not just the land was revived but the people were too. That is what living water does for the soul: it revives us. It is healing, and life sustaining, and filling. —EBF

Reflect and Respond

How does the living water of Christ revive you?

Your favorite scripture in Ether 9

ETHER 10:1

**Wherefore, Shez began to build
up again a broken people.**

Because of a famine that swept through the land, Shez's father, King Heth, and everyone else in his whole family except for Shez were killed. I cannot imagine what that must have been like. Heth, his father, was not a good man. He commanded that if any prophets came into the land they should either be kicked out of the city or thrown into a pit until they starved to death. When the king and the rest of his family died, Shez "began to build up again a broken people." Some reading the story might consider Shez himself a broken person. He came from both an unrighteous home and tragedy. He was not raised to believe in God or in His power to heal and build, but he remembered the story of the Lord building and healing the family of the brother of Jared, and that is where he took his cues from. Jared and his family had come out of a wicked place too, and the Lord had strengthened them and led them to a promised land. Perhaps the Lord could and would do the same for him. All Shez needed to do was begin again.

With God, the story is never over. It does not matter the past or circumstances that people came from. Like Shez, they can begin again. And not only can they begin again, they can be a force for good in building up others. I have witnessed this before. I have seen someone dear to me come from a broken place, break the pattern of unrighteousness in her family, and then spend her life building up others in righteousness. You can do it too. —DB

Reflect and Respond

What places do you see in your life, family, and friends where you can begin again to build up a broken situation?

Your favorite scripture in Ether 10

ETHER 11:17

And it came to pass that
there arose another mighty man . . .

I am a great admirer of the prophets.

It started when I was in junior high. I attended the viewing of President Spencer W. Kimball with a good friend and his mother. I will never forget the pictures we saw as we waited in line. As I passed by each of them and then through the place where he was, the Spirit impressed upon my soul, "This was a remarkable man." I was fifteen.

President Ezra Taft Benson followed in his steps. He taught me to love the Book of Mormon. My boys grew up with pictures of Book of Mormon scenes hanging on the walls of our home because that was what President Benson asked us to do.

President Howard W. Hunter taught me to love the temple.

President Gordon B. Hinckley was the prophet of my children's teenage years. We had only one rule in our home: whatever the prophet said, we did it. My kids grew up poring over his talks in order to govern their lives. I love that man for helping me raise my children.

President Thomas S. Monson taught me about the rescue. He helped me understand the importance of individual ministry and of loving the one. He is a prophet who won my heart because I witnessed him living what he preached.

When President Monson died, I prepared my heart to begin again, *and it came to pass that there arose another mighty man . . .* —EBF

Reflect and Respond
What do you love most about President Russell M. Nelson?

Your favorite scripture in Ether 11

ETHER 12:41

And now, I would commend you to **seek this Jesus**
of whom the prophets and apostles have written, that the
grace of God . . . may be and abide in you forever.

After summarizing the war-torn history of the Jaredites, a story that ended in destruction but was also full of miracles, Moroni gave future readers like you and me this simple bit of advice: "Seek this Jesus." Which Jesus? The one "whom the prophets and apostles have written" about. The one they gave their wealth, time, and everything for. Seek for Him. He is the answer every time.

This is the advice I want my kids to leave home with. I don't care if they know how to jump-start a car, apply for a loan, or plant a peach tree. They can Google those things. What I want them to know is that they can rely on Jesus in all situations. It is the advice I want to give to my friends. It is the advice I would give you with any problem or difficulty you are facing. Seek this Jesus. Because when you do, the "grace of God" will "be and abide in your forever." Jesus is strength. He is compassion. He is second chances. He is grace. He is God. —DB

Reflect and Respond

What are the ways you will teach your children, friends, and family to seek this Jesus?

Your favorite
scripture in
Ether 12

ETHER 13:10

And then cometh the New Jerusalem; and blessed
are they who dwell therein, for it is they whose garments
are **white through the blood of the Lamb**.

Have you ever washed a load of whites with one red sock? The damage is irreparable. Those white things will never be white again. It is a law of nature; I am sure of it. But Moroni tells us otherwise.

When all the war is ended and all the sin has gone away, the world will become a New Jerusalem—a holy place where the King of kings rules and reigns. I cannot wait for this day. I can't help but wonder who will be the citizens of this new kingdom, because Moroni said, "Blessed are they who dwell therein." Who are the lucky ones? It will be "they whose garments are white through the blood of the Lamb." I love Alma's use of the same analogy—"They were called after this holy order, and were sanctified, and their garments were washed white through the blood of the Lamb" (Alma 13:11). Are you picturing this? Can you imagine dipping some material into blood and having it come out white? Red blood on white fabric is the worst combination. Red stains deeply and permanently. To see something washed in blood come out sparkling white would shock me. It would leave me amazed—the same way grace always does. Those who dwell in this new heaven with Jesus are not people who lived perfect lives, but those who allowed Him to wash them clean in His blood. They are people who had mistakes and rebellions and sins and were changed deeply and permanently by Him. —DB

Reflect and Respond

Do you believe and accept this about your own sins: that you can be washed white and have a place in the New Jerusalem?

Your favorite scripture in Ether 13

ETHER 14:20

. . . and they were divided . . .

I have a rule about movies with sad endings. I don't watch them. Ever. My kids know this about me. They warn me about the sad endings. "Mom will hate that movie," they say as they make their weekend plans. They protect me from the sad ones. It's true about books, too. I have to know the ending before I begin. If it is sad, I can't read it. That's my rule. Maybe it's because life is sad enough already. My heart and my prayers and the worries that keep me up at night are all my soul can handle. When I go to a movie or read a book, I want to experience the happy ending.

With that in mind, I won't have to explain in detail how much I dislike the end of the Book of Mormon. I am sad about the wars, and the letting go of the Lord, and the division. The people were so happy until they got caught up in the division.

The lesson is not lost on me. I realize that one of the quickest ways to lose the Spirit is through contention, dissension, and division. I find myself becoming extra vigilant in that regard. We live in a time of discord. Voices of anger call on every side. One tweet can draw hundreds of people into a heated conversation. It is part of our culture now. It is becoming a way of life.

My greatest goal is to make sure that culture does not make its way into my home. I want there to be one place in this world that is safe, kind, and full of love and compassion, with as many happy endings as possible here in mortality. A place of peace. —EBF

Reflect and Respond
How are you learning to combat division in your home?

Your favorite scripture in Ether 14

ETHER 15:34

Now the last words which are written by Ether are these: Whether the
Lord will that I be translated, or that I suffer the will of the Lord in the flesh,
it mattereth not, **if it so be that I am saved in the kingdom of God**.

Have you ever agreed to something with an "as long as" condition on the agreement? I will go "as long as" so-and-so comes with us. Or, I can make it "as long as" I don't have to finish my other project. Usually the condition implies that no matter what else happens, you are agreeing as long as the one or two simple qualifications are met. When Jenny and I were looking for a house, I told her I would move into any house that she wanted. "Any?" she asked. "Well," I answered, "as long as it has two bathrooms upstairs and a separate closet room for the toilet in ours. That's it. I don't care about anything else." Some other things may have been annoying or not as convenient or nice, but I had only two conditions that mattered most to me. Trivial? Yes. Important? To me.

What are the "as long as" conditions that you have on your spirituality or hopes for your eternal future? What matters most? For Ether, at the end of his life, most of the things of the world stopped mattering to him. He wondered how he would leave the earth eventually—be translated or die—but it didn't matter to him. The only thing he wanted was to be "saved in the kingdom of God." That's it. —DB

Reflect and Respond

*What about you? Fill in the blank. It doesn't matter what else
happens to me in this life, as long as . . .*

Your favorite
scripture in
Ether 15

MORONI 1:3

And I, Moroni, will not deny the Christ . . .

The book of Moroni was an unplanned book. We know because Moroni begins it by saying that he hadn't planned on writing any more, but since he hadn't perished, he decided to write again. The last ten chapters of the Book of Mormon contain important truths about how to administer the sacrament; a sermon on faith, hope, and charity; the way Church meetings should be run; and a testimony of the Book of Mormon. However, one of the reasons I am most grateful Moroni wrote one last time is a line found in Moroni 1:3, "And I, Moroni, will not deny the Christ."

It is a statement of allegiance. A declaration of loyalty. A standing firm when all the world around him was falling apart.

It has been prophesied that in the last days many will fall away. "For there shall arise false Christs, and false prophets, and shall shew great signs and wonders; insomuch that, if it were possible, they shall deceive the very elect" (Matthew 24:24). And again in 2 Thessalonians 2:2, "That ye be not soon shaken in mind, or be troubled, neither by spirit, nor by word, nor by letter as from us, as that the day of Christ is at hand."

"Stand fast," Paul tells us, "and hold the traditions which ye have been taught" (2 Thessalonians 2:15). Paul talks about the conditions of the last days, that there won't just be a falling away, it will be a standing against, a defection, a battle. Where will you and I stand? I hope we will stand fast just as Moroni did, and say both in word and in action, "I will not deny the Christ." —EBF

. . . .

Reflect and Respond

Read "In His Steps," by President Ezra Taft Benson (Ensign, September 1988) and record your feelings. Where will you stand?

Your favorite scripture in Moroni 1

MORONI 2:2

And he called them by name . . .

The very first word spoken by God the Father in this dispensation was "Joseph." Everything else He would teach and reveal to the Prophet over the unfolding years of the Restoration would be eternally significant, but I wonder if Joseph always held on to the feeling he had when God spoke his name.

I have taught so many students over the years in high school seminary and college institute classes, and I run into them everywhere I go. If it has been quite a few years, they will usually start by asking me, "Do you remember me?" Happily, I have a pretty good memory, and most of the time I can give a sincere and enthusiastic, "Yes!" Even if I don't remember their names. One time, a past student walked up to me and started with the typical, "Do you remember me?" After I said, "Yes!" he shot back with, "Then what is my name? Do you remember it?" I was devastated, because the answer was no. I spent the next few minutes guessing it because he wouldn't tell me until I did. It was so awkward, and I was embarrassed I couldn't remember the young man's name. Luckily someone passed by and said hello to him and said his name, so I was let off the hook. I then said, "Sorry I didn't remember your name. But God does."

Even though that might be just a phrase I used to smooth over the situation, I actually believe it. I know He knows my name, and I cannot wait to hear His voice speak it. It will be music to me. I look forward to that day with great anticipation. —DB

Reflect and Respond

When is the last time you have felt like God knew you personally? Like He was calling your name?

Your favorite scripture in Moroni 2

MORONI 3:4

And after this manner did they ordain priests and teachers,
according to the gifts and callings of God unto men.

When I walked in through the gate and scanned the backyard, I felt like I was seeing what God hoped our lives would look like. Our next-door neighbor and friend was unexpectedly diagnosed with a dangerous illness. Immediately she began treatments and procedures to save her life. Almost instinctively, neighbors started brainstorming how we could lift the burden. "I wish there was something we could do" was not normally the personality of our street, but it was the beginning of spring, and she loved a beautiful yard, and the sickness made her bed bound. So we got to work. Some were expert in sprinkler systems. Others knew how to trim trees. One neighbor had an eye for choosing the perfect flowers, and I knew how to hold open a garbage sack. I ran out to the front yard to get an extra big black bag, and when I walked back through the gate and scanned the backyard, I saw all of our neighbors and friends scattered there, each one busily doing a different job. Each was working and helping according to the skill he or she had. Together, we turned her backyard into a masterpiece. I think this is what God hoped would happen with our lives. He would send gifts and callings to each of us, hoping we would gather together and use them in a way to turn this ordinary experience of mortality into a masterpiece. —DB

Reflect and Respond

What do you feel called to, or what gifts do you feel like the Lord has gifted you with? How are you using them to fulfill great purposes?

Your favorite scripture in Moroni 3

MORONI 4:3

**. . . that they are willing to take
upon them the name of thy Son . . .**

A friend of mine called me after he left sacrament meeting one Sunday to tell me a question that had popped into his mind while he was listening to the sacrament prayers. As the priesthood holders repeated the same prayer that Moroni wrote in the last chapters of the Book of Mormon, he heard the phrase, "that they are willing to take upon them the name of thy Son." As soon as he heard them say it, the thought came to his mind, "But which name?" He and I had been talking back and forth for weeks about the different names and titles of Jesus Christ that are used throughout the scriptures. There are more than one hundred unique and different names of Him contained there. The Lamb of God. The Advocate. King of kings. Redeemer. The Holy One of Israel. During the ordinance of the sacrament, we promise to take upon us His name. This phrase has many meanings, but my friend started to wonder what it would mean for him to take on one of the names of Christ. What if he lived as an advocate for others that week? What if he spoke with more holiness? What if he lived a sacrificial week like the Lamb? It turned into a pattern. Each week, he listened to the prayer and then chose a different name of Jesus. He studied it out in scripture and then tried to live that week according to what he had learned and felt. It has led to a closeness with Jesus and a love for each of His names. —DB

Reflect and Respond
Which name of Jesus has the most meaning to you?

Your favorite
scripture in
Moroni 4

MORONI 5:2

...that they may witness unto thee, O God,
the Eternal Father, **that they do always remember
him**, that they may have his Spirit to be with them.

Sometimes I wonder if other people have as many moments of weakness and doubt as I do. There are times when life gets hard. Other times I am embarrassed at the level of my faith or the desires of my heart. As much as I don't want to, I cannot believe how often I backslide into sin I thought I had left behind, and temptation seems to be heavier than normal some days. My friend gave me a sticker once that said, "Y'all need Jesus." She thought I would like it. She was right. I did. But she probably didn't know how much I would need Jesus, or how much I needed the reminder on those days.

Each week we promise to remember the Savior. Not because He needs remembering, but because we need Him. And when I think of Him—when I remember His life, miracles, ministry, and sacrifice for me—it fills me with strength. One particular scene from His life that I love to remember is the first Christmas morning. I picture sweet Mary holding Him tenderly in her arms. I see the shepherds kneeling and the star beaming. This picture moves me deeply. I remember that He gave up His throne on high to come to earth—into my mess—to rescue me. When I picture this—when I remember Him— I feel a surge of His Spirit. And that Spirit gives me strength and hope and reassurance. Every time. —DB

Reflect and Respond

What can you do to more often think of and remember Jesus?

Your favorite
scripture in
Moroni 5

MORONI 6:4

They were numbered among the people of the church of Christ; and their names were taken, that they might be remembered and nourished by the good word of God.

Jenny and I have six kids, and sometimes it feels like a hundred to us. We ended up buying a huge van we named Rosa that has fifteen seats, looks like an airport shuttle, and is tall enough to stand up in, with an aisle to walk down the middle. The seats are all just high enough that for most of the kids we can see only tufts of hair when we look through the rearview mirror. After everyone piles in after Sunday dinner at my aunt's house, we have to have everyone count off to make sure they are all there. As much as it would be nice to have someone else put them to bed at night, we want to make sure we don't forget any of them when we leave.

If strangers were to watch this count off occur, they might not know what was happening, and perhaps they would consider it a cold and technical way of looking after people—to treat them like numbers. If that were the only moment of our life they saw, that would be all they would hear. But when I hear each number called, it means something more. I know number one's name. I know his favorite color and cereal and baseball team. I know what gets him annoyed, and I know what his specific needs are. The number simply helps me keep track of him. It helps me remember not to forget him, so he can be nourished and watched over by his father. —DB

Reflect and Respond

Is there someone you know who might be forgotten right now? Is there a way you could remember them and nourish them in God?

Your favorite scripture in Moroni 2

MORONI 7:46

Charity never faileth.

The woman sitting next to me on the flight from Florida had the softest eyes I've ever seen. Her hands rested gently on the white cowboy hat sitting on her lap. Of course, I asked about Hurricane Irma. She told me about her daughter and her two tiny boys, still there. And her mother. How they would sleep in the hallway tonight, away from the windows, sheltered together from the storm. We spoke of her son, who had been injured in combat. Her husband, who one day packed up and walked away for another woman. How she started her own construction business and how she made it, is still making it, even now.

I looked into those kind, dark eyes and said I was sorry her life had been so hard. "It's okay," she told me. "It's the way it should be. The hard things have taught me to be more compassionate to those who will walk that same road one day. Every time a trial comes, it simply reminds me that now I have more to give." Those soft eyes filled with wisdom just then, and I realized I had just been handed a truth I never want to forget. Those hard days, all those hard things, they have helped each one of us have more to give.

When I think of charity, I think of Christ, who taught us the true meaning of love. Sometimes, just remembering His love for me and the sacrifice He gave for me is all it takes to remind me that I have so much more to give. When I love in His name, it becomes an expression of charity, of His love. And His love never runs out, never gives up, and never ever fails. He always has more to give. —EBF

Reflect and Respond
What do you know about the love of Christ?

Your favorite scripture in Moroni 7

MORONI 8:2

My beloved son, Moroni, I rejoice exceedingly that your Lord Jesus Christ hath been mindful of you, **and hath called you to his ministry**, and to his holy work.

This is a line from a letter that Mormon, Moroni's dad, wrote to him as a missionary. He had just been called to the ministry, and this was evidently one of the first letters that Moroni received. I loved that first letter I got from my dad in the MTC. I wonder if Moroni opened it with the same vigor and cried the same kind of tears that I did. My dad had been there before—in the ministry—so I felt like it connected us. The same was true for Moroni.

Many years later, I was at the Provo MTC again, but this time to drop off my brother-in-law, Justin. When the time came for everyone to say their good-byes, Justin was going down the row giving everyone his last hugs. I was pretty proud of myself because I cannot usually keep it together emotionally for any type of good-bye, particularly a missionary one. But this time I was doing great, until I turned around. In the row right next to us there was a teary-eyed, brown-haired missionary who was saying good-bye too. Because of where my chair was, I was just about two feet away from him when his dad pulled him in close for a tender embrace. I heard them both sniffle, and I felt my eyes start to well up too. And then the dad whispered in the boy's ear, "I love you, son. I'm so proud of you." Perhaps the father knew what a beautiful thing this holy work and call to the ministry would be—just like Mormon did when he wrote to Moroni and my dad did when he wrote to me. —DB

Reflect and Respond

Who has sustained you in your ministry? What did it mean to you?

Your favorite scripture in Moroni 8

MORONI 9:26

And **may the grace of God the Father**, whose throne is high in the heavens, and our Lord Jesus Christ, who sitteth on the right hand of his power, until all things shall become subject unto him, **be, and abide with you forever**.

When I was called into a leadership position in our ward, I was given some advice that shaped everything I did. One of the things I was a little nervous about was my inability to help people solve their problems. I was young and inexperienced and knew I would face situations in which I wouldn't know what to do or how to help. My friend and fellow leader said to me, "Do not try to carry a burden that God has already carried. Your job isn't to fix or change people—that is His. Your job is to breathe hope into the situation."

I love the description of both God the Father and the Son in this verse that comes from a letter of advice that Mormon wrote to his son. Perhaps he knew that his son would feel this same level of inadequacy as he tried to minister to his people. Mormon reminded Moroni that God's throne is high in the heavens—above and over all things— that His Son sits next to Him in power, and that one day "all things shall become subject unto him." They have the knowledge and power and ability to solve all things. Every one. And one day They will. Until then, trust Them, look to Them, and abide in Their grace. There is hope in that place. And it is the perfect place to wait for all things to work out for good. —DB

Reflect and Respond

Have you sensed the strength that comes from this sort of perspective? How do you abide in His grace in times of trouble?

Your favorite scripture in Moroni 9

MORONI 10:6

And whatsoever thing is good is just and true.

The last chapter of the Book of Mormon is a chapter that a lot of people turn to when they are seeking to know and learn truth. There is a promise from Moroni that those who seek to know truth, particularly about the Book of Mormon itself, can remember the goodness of God, read, study it out, and then pray for a witness that it is true. This is his promise to all who seek for their own conviction. "By the power of the Holy Ghost ye may know the truth of all things" (Moroni 10:5).

But what if someone doesn't know whether something is true yet? What if they feel like they can't stand before a congregation or say with conviction that they know for sure that God is real, that the Book of Mormon or Bible is true, that they know that the prophets are truly called of God, or that the Church is Jesus's restored Church on the earth? What if they don't *know*? This is why I love Moroni's next teaching in his promise: "And whatsoever thing is good is . . . true." What if I can't say I know something is true, but I do know that it is good? What if I *can* stand before a congregation and say with conviction that I know that God is good? Or I might not know the Book of Mormon is true, but I do know that it teaches good things. Or what if I'm not sure if the prophets are called of God, but I believe they are good men? And this church—I know it is a good, good church.

What if you started there? What if the process of discovering truth simply begins by just asking if something is good? —DB

Reflect and Respond

Take some time to look back over your scriptures and the notes and feelings you wrote down this year. What do you know is good?

Your favorite scripture in Moroni 10

CONCLUSION

We have finished a full-year study of the Book of Mormon and, as it comes to a close, we want to invite you to do three things.

First, at the beginning of the Book of Mormon, Nephi invites every reader to consider the tender mercies of the Lord that are over all those whom He has chosen because of their faith. Tender mercies to make us mighty and to deliver us. Have you witnessed those tender mercies in your life this year? If you haven't already, take some time to write those down so that you will always remember them. (We've provided some journaling pages in the back of this book if you want to put those thoughts there.)

Second, many prophets have testified of the promised blessings that come from reading the Book of Mormon. We encourage you to search out these promises, read through them, and write down the ones you have experienced over the course of this year.

Last, we want to remind you of the introduction to this book. Do you remember the trip to Disneyland with the tour guide in the checkered vest? As our family left Disneyland that day, our guide had us stop at a small building at the end of Main Street before leaving the park. He pointed out a red brick building with a bell on top. On the second floor there is one window with the shade half drawn and a lamp centered in the middle. The lamp is always on. It is a reminder that the spirit of Walt Disney is always there. It reminds me of the introduction to the Book of Mormon, a book that is another testament of Jesus Christ, who manifests Himself unto all, who shows unto each of us great things, who is always there. The Book of Mormon was written to draw us nearer to Him. Perhaps you could take some time to write down your testimony of Jesus Christ and His personal ministry in your story.

The Book of Mormon ends with an invitation for all of us: "Come unto Christ, and be perfected in him, . . . and love God with all your might, mind and strength" (Moroni 10:32). That is what we have done this year. May that continue to be our journey in the years to come.

ABOUT THE AUTHORS

Photo by Hunter Fowler

EMILY BELLE FREEMAN is a best-selling author and popular inspirational speaker. She has a deep love of the scriptures, which comes from a desire to find their application in everyday life. She is the author of numerous books, including *Creating a Christ-Centered Home; Closer to Christ;* and *Even This: Getting to the Place Where You Can Trust God with Anything.* She is a favorite speaker at Time Out for Women and a cohost with David Butler of *Don't Miss This,* a "Come, Follow Me" study channel on YouTube. Her greatest joy comes from spending time with her family. Read more at emilybellefreeman.com and follow Emily on Instagram and Facebook @emilybellefreeman.

Photo by Nikki Davis

DAVID BUTLER'S greatest love is people. He has adopted as a life motto: "Stuff no mattah, people mattah." His favorite people are his wife, Jenny, and their six darling children. Some of his other loves include good food, spontaneous adventures, Christmas morning, and the sea. David cohosts the popular YouTube scripture study channel *Don't Miss This* with Emily Belle Freeman and is the author of many religious books, including *Ites: An Illustrated Guide to the People in the Book of Mormon; The Peter Potential;* and *Almighty: How the Most Powerful Being in the Universe Is Also Your Loving Father.* Follow him on Instagram @ mrdavebutler.